COLLINS GEM
ANTIQUE
MARKS

COLLINS GEM
BIBLE
GUIDE

COLLINS GEM
Body
LANGUAGE

COLLINS GEM
CARD
Games

COLLINS G
CRICKE

GW00391134

EM
ID

COLLINS GEM
INTERNET

COLLINS GEM
PREDICTING

COLLINS GEM
Ready
REFERENCE

COLLINS GEM
SHARKS

COLLINS GEM
WHALES
& DOLPHINS

COLLINS GEM
WHISKY

COLLINS GEM
WORD
PROCESSING

COLLINS GEM
Your PC

The right of Brian Laban to be identified as the author of this work has been asserted by him in accordance with the Copyright, Designs and Patents Act 1988

HarperCollins*Publishers*
Westerhill Road, Bishopbriggs, Glasgow G64 2QT

First published 2000

Reprint 10 9 8 7 6 5 4 3 2 1 0

The author and publisher have made every reasonable effort to contact all copyright holders. Any errors that may have occurred are inadvertent and anyone who for any reason has not been contacted is invited to write to the publisher so that a full acknowledgment may be made in subsequent editions of this work.

ISBN 0 00 472475-5

Printed in Italy by Amadeus S.p.A.

Contents

Introduction

When Karl Benz rolled out the world's first successful petrol-engined automobile, in 1886, it had three wheels, one cylinder, 954cc and around 0.8hp at the heady speed of 250 to 300rpm. With a tail wind and a level road, it might achieve 10mph – but then speed wasn't so important as the fact that it ran at all. That attitude wasn't going to last.

After Benz, the pioneers came thick and fast, all wanting to make their spin on the automobile better than the last. It took a while for the car to be faster than the horse, even longer for it to be faster than the railways, but in 1899 Camille Jenatzy became the first motorist to exceed 100kph and by 1904 the record had passed 100mph. The early record breakers were generally based on the early racing cars, and what they learned filtered back into everyday motoring. Ordinary cars went faster and a new breed sprang up even before World War I – the sports car. But it wasn't only sports cars that grew sportier; saloons and coupés and cabrios all came in on the act, and they've been going faster ever since. Not just faster in top speed but faster to accelerate, faster around corners, even faster to stop. Here are some of the fastest.

AC Shelby Cobra

Dates built: 1962–69

The AC Shelby Cobra is probably the most imitated car of all time, for its looks, its performance and its simplicity. It was conceived by flamboyant Texan Carroll Shelby, former racing driver and 1959 Le Mans winner. In 1961 he married Ford's lightweight V8 engine with an uprated version of AC's Ace chassis and by July 1963 the Cobra was in production. Its nimble European chassis and low-cost American horsepower made the Cobra one of the fastest-accelerating sports cars of all time, a successful racing car and a sports car icon. Its original 289cu

SPECIFICATIONS	Model Year 1963
Engine type:	**Ford V8**
Capacity/power:	**4.7 litres/271bhp**
Top speed (mph):	**137**
0–60mph (secs):	**4.3**

in (4.7-litre) engine gave 271bhp in the mildest road cars or almost 400bhp in the wildest racers, in a car weighing barely 2000lb. On the road it would hit 60mph in around four seconds and nudge 140mph. For racing it was even quicker, and a winner everywhere. In 1965 the Daytona, a more aerodynamic coupé version of the 289 Cobra, beat Ferrari to the world sports car championship. The same year Shelby launched a 427cu in (7-litre) version, which was bigger and faster. Although 425bhp was normal, 800bhp was possible – the latter giving Shelby's own car 0–100mph in 7.9 seconds, in 1968!

Alfa Romeo 8C Monza

Dates built: 1931–39

From 1931 until production ended with the war in 1939, the 8C was Alfa's sporting heart. In various forms it was a Grand Prix winner on circuits from Monaco to Monza, a four times Le Mans winner and a superb sports car. Designed by legendary engineer Vittorio Jano (enticed to Alfa's racing department in 1923 by team manager Enzo Ferrari), it debuted as a long-wheelbase 2.3-litre sports car and in May 1931 won the Targa Florio. Two weeks later, in stripped, short-chassis form, 8Cs finished first and second in the Italian GP at Monza, giving the rare short-chassis racer its name. Powered by Jano's glorious supercharged twin-cam straight-eight engine, it grew to 2.6 litres for racing (and some customer cars) and featured in the classic Monza. For the road the 8C 2300 had around

SPECIFICATIONS	Model Year 1938
Engine type:	**in-line 8-cyl**
Capacity/power:	**2.6 litres/180bhp**
Top speed (mph):	**135**
0–60mph (secs):	**7.0**

140bhp; for racing the 2600 had as much as 180bhp, with great reliability. On the road, the race-bred Monza, with its ladder chassis and all-round cart springs, is reasonably comfortable, amazingly agile and precise, and very quick, with a top speed of around 135mph and 0–60mph in 7 seconds – which would not disgrace many sporty cars more than sixty years on.

Alfa Romeo SZ

Dates built: 1989–93

Alfa described the outrageous SZ as their
'alternative supercar', a wonderfully apt
description for one of the most distinctive road
cars to be produced in the late 1980s. However,
the SZ wasn't only about looks. From its
conception in 1987 to its show debut just two
years later in 1989, the development programme
was as fast as the car itself. The styling of the two-
door, two-seater coupé was the result of a two-
team in-house competition and the SZ was to be
built by Milanese coachbuilder Zagato, in a
limited series of 1000. Nominally it shared the
chassis of the 75 saloon, with the 75's wheelbase,
front engine and rear transaxle, but it also had
a very stiff steel shell onto which the plastic
panels were bonded for even greater stiffness.
Suspension was derived from the 75 Evoluzione

SPECIFICATIONS	Model Year 1989
Engine type:	**V6**
Capacity/power:	**3.0 litres/210bhp**
Top speed (mph):	**150**
0–60mph (secs):	**6.9**

racer, special tyres were supplied by Pirelli and
the car was aggressively low and aerodynamic.
Power came from a 210bhp version of Alfa's
glorious 3-litre V6, and although a top speed of
just over 150mph and 0–60mph in just under
7 seconds were not quite supercar quick, they
were only a part of the SZ's appeal – the real
beauty of the car was in its sensational balance,
superb grip and lightning responses. And, of
course, those looks.

Allard J2

Dates built: 1950–54

Long before Carroll Shelby conceived the Cobra,
Sydney Allard was making a speciality of putting
off-the-shelf American horsepower into European
sports car chassis, for maximum performance
with minimum cost and complexity. Allard, a
south London Ford dealer and enthusiastic trials
driver, built a handful of cars before World War
II with sidevalve Ford V8s and even Lincoln
V12 engines, and, after the war, started small-
scale production of usually Ford V8-powered
saloons and sports cars. In 1952 he won the
Monte Carlo Rally in one of his own cars, and was
selling Allards to the United States. These might
be powered by one of a number of different
engines – Ford, Cadillac or Chrysler engines –
but they always had the same characteristic of
big engine in a fairly light and simple chassis.

S P E C I F I C A T I O N S	Model Year 1954
Engine type:	**Ford/Chrysler/Cadillac V8**
Capacity/power:	**5.4 litres/230bhp (Chrysler)**
Top speed (mph):	**120+**
0–60mph (secs):	**8.0**

Allard launched his most famous model, the J2, in 1950. It was based on one of his hillclimb specials, with a two-seater body and cycle-type front wings. It had a fairly sophisticated de Dion rear suspension but a much cruder independent front suspension, using a centrally split beam axle. What made it special, though, was plenty of horsepower from a Ford or Cadillac V8 of 5.5 litres or more, and very little weight. A simple formula, but a foolproof one.

Alpine A110

Dates built: 1963–74

The Alpine marque was born out of motor sport, made good as a production car manufacturer, but never strayed far from its racing roots. Its founder was Jean Redele, a Renault dealer from Dieppe who started tuning small Renaults for his own racing purposes before moving on to building Renault-powered sports cars for a growing market. Redele's most famous and successful model (in competition at least) was the beautiful Alpine A110, which he manufactured from 1963 to 1974, during which time he also ran Renault's official competition programme. The first A110 used a four-cylinder Renault engine of less than 1 litre and a four-speed gearbox, but over the years gear-count grew to five and capacity through 1.3 and 1.6 and finally to 1.8 litres, while power reached around

SPECIFICATIONS	Model Year 1973
Engine type:	**Renault in-line 4-cyl**
Capacity/power:	**1.6 litres/138bhp**
Top speed (mph):	**127**
0–60mph (secs):	**6.2**

170bhp for the 1.8 competition version that took the World Rally Championship in 1973, after dozens of major rally successes over the years, including the prestigious Monte Carlo. The A110 used a tubular steel backbone chassis, a rear-mounted engine and swing-axle rear suspension, which could make it quite nervous when pushed hard, but rally drivers were comfortable with that, while road car buyers loved the rally car looks and performance.

Aston Martin DB4GT

Dates built: 1959–63

The Aston DB4GT had a famous party trick:
it could blast from 0–100mph and back to zero
again in less than 20 seconds, which, in 1959
when it was first launched, was a considerable
achievement, as was 0–60mph in 6.4 seconds.
The DB4GT was developed from the softer and
more luxurious DB4, but the new car was very
different from its predecessor. The wheelbase was
5 inches shorter, dispensing with the small rear
seats in favour of luggage space, while the boot
housed a new 30-gallon petrol tank and the spare
wheel. It had a new, rounded nose with flared-in
headlights. It had simpler trim and plexiglass rear
windows, making it 180lb lighter than the DB4.
The new car was also far more powerful. The 3.7-
litre twin-cam straight-six had increased
compression, new camshafts, three twin-choke

SPECIFICATIONS	Model Year 1960
Engine type:	**in-line 6-cyl**
Capacity/power:	**3.7 litres/302bhp**
Top speed (mph):	**150+**
0–60mph (secs):	**6.4**

Weber carburettors and twin plugs per cylinder,
raising its output to 302bhp, which woofled and
growled through a special exhaust system. It was
a car for strong and brave drivers. The build
quality was hewn-from-solid, the controls were
heavy, its handling balanced but demanding skill,
and its performance ferocious, up to a maximum
of over 150mph. The Aston Martin DB4GT was a
Grand Tourer in the finest sense and in the
Zagato-bodied version (pictured) is renowned as
one of the most desirable Astons of all.

Aston Martin Vantage 600

Dates built: 1999–on

The clue is in the name: 600bhp and 600lb ft of torque made the 1999 Vantage 600 the most powerful production car in the world and, in spite of its size and weight, one of the fastest. The special version of Aston's long-running GT had the hand-built quality of any Vantage, but it also had a 'Works Prepared' 5.3-litre V8 with four camshafts, 32 valves and two superchargers. That produced an earth-shaking soundtrack but also gave the muscular front-engined, rear-drive 2+2 coupé a claimed maximum of more than 200mph, with 0–60mph

SPECIFICATIONS	Model Year 1999
Engine type:	**V8**
Capacity/power:	**5.3 litres/600bhp**
Top speed (mph):	**200+**
0–60mph (secs):	**4.4**

in less than 4.5 seconds and 100mph in less than ten – and at that speed it was barely into its long-legged stride. It also had the manners to match its performance, thanks to 285/45 tyres on huge 18-inch wheels, retuned suspension with stiffer springs and dampers, and racing-specification brakes with enormous discs on all four wheels and ABS with electronic stability control. It was a big car with big personality, big power and big performance. At almost £250,000 it also had a fairly big price tag, but at least it had four seats.

Audi Sport quattro

Dates built: 1983–85

With the original quattro Audi introduced a
performance twist that stood the rallying world
on its head. Previously, four-wheel drive had
mainly meant mud-plugging versatility. The
quattro, however, used this to give stunning
traction and roadholding in a sporting car, and
thus created a new genre. In 1983, for Group B
rallying (which brought 500bhp cars and near
F1 performance to the forests but was soon
banned as too dangerous), Audi launched the
Sport quattro. It was ten inches shorter than the
original, on a 12.6-inch shorter wheelbase, and
therefore more nimble. Strangely, it was slightly
heavier, but it was also more powerful. To qualify
for motor sport it had to be a production
model – although the output was small and very
expensive. It had a turbocharged five-cylinder

SPECIFICATIONS	Model Year 1983
Engine type:	**in-line 5-cyl**
Capacity/power:	**2.1 litres/306bhp**
Top speed (mph):	**155**
0–60mph (secs):	**4.5**

20-valve engine giving 306bhp in road trim, enough to blast the car to 60mph in 4.5 seconds, 100mph in 12.5 seconds and to a maximum of 155mph. Oddly, it didn't work well in rallying and was considered difficult to drive, but as a road car the Sport quattro was wonderful – superbly trimmed with full leather upholstery, virtually temperament-free, yet with staggering straightline performance and handling, and roadholding that made its bigger brother feel positively cumbersome.

Audi RS2

Dates built: 1994–95

The Audi RS2 is an estate car that thinks it's a supercar. Launched in 1994, the RS2 was a limited-edition range-topper, developed by Porsche. It looked the part, too – it sat low and chunky on 17-inch five-spoke Porsche Cup racing series wheels, through which you could see huge brake discs and red-painted calipers borrowed from the Porsche 968 Club Sport. Power – lots of it – came from a tuned version of the 'ordinary' S2's turbocharged 2.2-litre five-cylinder 20-valve engine. With new camshafts, a much bigger turbo and higher boost, it pushed output to a mighty 315bhp. That was kept in check by the massive tyres as well as by the latest generation of Audi's quattro four-wheel-drive system, so the RS2 had excellent grip, very protective manners (even if you were heading for

SPECIFICATIONS   Model Year 1994

Engine type:	**in-line 5-cyl**
Capacity/power:	**2.2 litres/315bhp**
Top speed (mph):	**163**
0–60mph (secs):	**5.2**

the ski slopes) and room in which to carry the
whole family – and maybe even the kitchen sink
if you felt so inclined. It didn't have quite the
tautness and steering responses of an out-and-out
sports car but it certainly had the performance.
With almost 165mph and 0–60mph in 5.2
seconds on tap, the RS2 might not have been the
world's most practical estate car, but it was
definitely the fastest.

Austin Healey 3000

Dates built: 1959–67

The Austin Healey 3000 was universally known as 'the big Healey', which perfectly describes its character. With its very similar predecessor, the 100 Six, it was BMC's rally car of choice until the arrival of the amazing Mini, and it was an archetypally English sports car. It was rugged rather than sophisticated but the formula worked. It was a good-looking two-seater (or 2+2) convertible with optional hardtop, and it ran from 1959 to 1967 with numerous alterations in detail but little change in its big-hearted character. The big heart was a fairly heavy but very reliable 3-litre straight-six engine with pushrod overhead valves and either two or three carburettors, depending on model. Power started at 124bhp but rose to 132 in the MkII, and 148 in the MkIII, giving the latter a maximum of just

SPECIFICATIONS	Model Year 1964
Engine type:	**in-line 6-cyl**
Capacity/power:	**3.0 litres/148bhp**
Top speed (mph):	**120+**
0–60mph (secs):	**9.8**

over 120mph. It was simple under the skin, too, with coil and wishbone front suspension, a live rear axle on semi-elliptic springs, front disc and rear drum brakes, and a four-speed manual gearbox with optional electric overdrive. It was a prolific rally winner, and its dependability was a plus point for road users. It was also comfortable, easy to live with and commercially successful.

Bentley 4¹/₂ Blower

Dates built: 1929–31

Mention Bentleys and Le Mans and most people might imagine the mighty 4¹/₂ 'Blower' thundering along the Mulsanne straight. But, surprisingly, this most famous Bentley never actually won Le Mans and what's more, the racing version wasn't even built by the Bentley factory.

W. O. Bentley hated supercharging and believed the way to more power was ever bigger engines. In 1929 Bentley driver Sir Henry 'Tim' Birkin disagreed. With the backing of the Honourable Dorothy Paget, he commissioned four supercharged racing versions of the unblown four-cylinder car. They were based on the overhead-camshaft, 16-valve, 4¹/₂-litre car that Bentley previewed at Le Mans in 1927 and that had won the race in 1928. While Bentley moved on to 6¹/₂ litres, the Birkin racers, built in a

SPECIFICATIONS	Model Year 1930
Engine type:	**in-line 4-cyl**
Capacity/power:	**4.5 litres/175 bhp**
Top speed (mph):	**130**
0–60mph (secs):	**n/a**

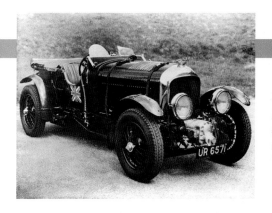

workshop in Welwyn Garden City, extensively redesigned the 4½-litre engine, added the famous supercharger on the nose, put on the classic open bodywork and started a legend.

Bentley's unblown version gave around 110bhp; the fifty 'production' supercharged tourers grudgingly built by Bentley between 1929 and 1931 gave 175bhp; Birkin's racing 'Blowers' had as much as 256bhp, and the two-ton car would nudge 130mph in Le Mans trim. This was enough for Birkin to lead the race in 1930 and to set a new lap record, but never to win.

Bentley Continental T

Dates built: 1996–on

The Bentley Continental T is a very unusual supercar, a 170mph gentleman's club whose astonishing performance completely belies its size, weight and luxurious accommodation. It may greet you with the smell of soft leather and the luxury of lambswool carpets, and it may weigh two and a half tons, but the Continental T is a Bentley in the classic mould of Le Mans winners and luxurious limousines. It only has two doors and is loosely described as a 'close-coupled' (that is, short-wheelbase) coupé, but it is a full four-seater and exquisitely equipped and refined. The twist is its giant performance. Its 6.7-litre V8 engine is relatively old-fashioned, with pushrod-operated valves and lazy delivery, but with a truck-sized turbocharger it raises 420bhp and no less than 650lb ft of torque – the most pulling

SPECIFICATIONS	Model Year 1996
Engine type:	**V8**
Capacity/power:	**6.7 litres/420bhp**
Top speed (mph):	**170**
0–60mph (secs):	**5.7**

power of any road car in the world. That helps it thunder to 60mph in only 5.7 seconds and on to at least 170mph, but even more surprising than the straightline performance is the fact that the battleship-sized Bentley is no wallowing barge. With huge tyres on beautiful alloy wheels, very well-developed suspension and superb brakes, the T surprises many a more obvious sports car.

Bentley W16 Hunaudières

Dates built: 1999 concept car

Bentley's rebirth as a truly sporting marque
started in the 1980s with cars like the Turbo, the
Mulsanne and the Continental, and continued
with rumours of a Bentley return to Le Mans in
the new millennium, promoted by Bentley's new
owners, Volkswagen.

At the Geneva Show in March 1999, Bentley
showed its first-ever mid-engined concept car,
and it was a supercar. Badged Hunaudières after
the famous Le Mans straight, it was super smooth
but at the same time was aggressively broad and
low and with a stance that crouched forwards. It
was powered by an incredible all-alloy 8-litre 16-
cylinder four-cam engine, in an impressively
compact W configuration. It promised 623bhp, a
maximum of more than 200mph and 0–60mph in
the four-second bracket.

SPECIFICATIONS	Model Year 1999
Engine type:	**W16**
Capacity/power:	**8.0 litres/623bhp**
Top speed (mph):	**200+**
0–60mph (secs):	**3.8**

The original 'technology testbed' as shown at Geneva was based on the four-wheel-drive platform of a Lamborghini Diablo VT. However, any production version would have its own chassis, with all the comforts a Bentley owner would demand, even in a supercar. That would include a five-speed automatic gearbox, and although the W16 dimensions were more compact than a Diablo, the Hunaudières offered generous passenger space, which was superbly trimmed and equipped to reflect the car's massive but effortless performance. Even in the world of supercars, Bentley's vision would be unique.

BMW 507

Dates built: 1955–59

After World War II, BMW was almost extinct.
By the 1950s it was fighting back and trying to
re-establish a sporting image last seen when the
328 won the 1940 Mille Miglia. In 1952 BMW
built its first postwar cars, and in 1955 it
launched the 507. It was an instant classic, which
borrowed most mechanical elements from the
saloon car line. The 3.2-litre V8 was upgraded
from the 502, with sporty camshaft, reworked
cylinder heads and twin carburettors, to give a
respectable and extremely refined 150bhp, up
to 135mph and 0–60mph in around 10 seconds.
The ladder-type chassis was based on the 503's,
with 14 inches chopped from the wheelbase.
Suspension is wishbones at the front and a live
axle with Panhard rod at the back, controlled by
long, slim torsion bars. The stunning bodywork

SPECIFICATIONS	Model Year 1957
Engine type:	**V8**
Capacity/power:	**3.2 litres/150bhp**
Top speed (mph):	**135**
0–60mph (secs):	**10.0**

was designed by Count Albrecht von Goertz, a German aristocrat working in New York, and the car was aimed very much at the American market. The 507 is lithe and muscular, with beautiful details, and just as impressive inside, mixing real comfort with classic sporting simplicity. It was expensive, and only 252 were built before it went out of production in 1959, but there are few better-looking cars.

BMW M1

Dates built: 1978–1981

The BMW M1 never remotely achieved the status it deserved. It had a troubled launch, delayed by production problems as a road car and missing the boat as a racing car because regulations had changed in the meantime.

When it did arrive, the BMW M1 was strangely overlooked and misunderstood, but it was actually one of the most capable, civilised and practical supercars of its generation. It was styled by Giugiaro and was as Teutonically understated as its Italian rivals were flamboyant. It was

SPECIFICATIONS	Model Year 1978
Engine type:	**in-line 6-cyl**
Capacity/power:	**3.5 litres/277bhp**
Top speed (mph):	**160+**
0–60mph (secs):	**5.5**

powered by a magnificent straight-six engine developed by BMW's Motorsport division – 3.5 litres developing a glorious-sounding 277bhp to propel the M1 past 160mph and to 60mph in only 5.5 seconds, with the most uncomplicated flexibility all across the speed range.

However, what set the M1 apart was its character, which was as far from the typical supercar rival as its looks. It was beautifully built, luxuriously trimmed, genuinely comfortable on almost any kind of road and had impeccable, drama-free handling up to extremely high limits. It was the perfect car for covering great distances in a serious hurry, and in many ways there were few other cars that could match it. If only more people had known.

BMW M5

Dates built: 1998–on

In BMW, the M badge stands for the Motorsport division and adorns the most exciting BMWs of all. The latest generation M5 is the most powerful BMW M car to date and the world's fastest five-seater saloon, but it is also a genuine luxury car and perfectly at home providing everyday transport. At its heart is an all-alloy 5-litre V8 with every power-enhancing trick in the Motorsport book. It has four overhead camshafts – all with variable valve timing – four valves per cylinder, racing style individual air-inlet controls, special oil and

SPECIFICATIONS	Model Year 1998
Engine type:	**V8**
Capacity/power:	**5.0 litres/400bhp**
Top speed (mph):	**155 (limited)**
0–60mph (secs):	**5.1**

cooling systems, and hugely sophisticated electronic engine management. Its 400bhp goes through a close-ratio six-speed manual gearbox to the rear wheels, reined in by wide, sticky tyres on ten-spoke, 18-inch alloy wheels, race-bred 'compound' disc brakes and by BMW's sophisticated Dynamic Stability Control. The latter maximises traction and handling balance by interactions between the engine management and ABS braking systems. Top speed is limited to 155mph but 0–60mph takes only 5.1 seconds and the M5 is quicker over a standing kilometre than a Porsche 911 – yet it is as luxurious and as understated as any other 5 Series.

BMW M Coupé

Dates built: 1998–on

BMW say they created the M Coupé simply because they could. The coupé is essentially a Z3 roadster with a roof and, once a low-budget after-hours project at the Z3 factory had proved it was possible, its future was assured. Launched in 1998, the M Coupé's styling is controversial, but BMW say it looks that way because that (as they worked out with cardboard and plastic foam mock-ups) was the easiest way to do it. Under the skin the car is all Z3 or, in the case of the M Coupé, all M Roadster. It has the M3 saloon's superb 321bhp 3.2-litre straight-six, with a five-speed gearbox because the M3's six-speeder won't fit. It has the Z3's strut front and semi-trailing arm rear suspension, lowered and stiffened for this ultimate performance version. That performance includes a limited

SPECIFICATIONS	Model Year 1998
Engine type:	**in-line 6-cyl**
Capacity/power:	**3.2 litres/321bhp**
Top speed (mph):	**155 (limited)**
0–60mph (secs):	**5.1**

155mph maximum, and 0–60mph in a blink over
5 seconds. As well as being very practical with its
big luggage area, the Coupé is quieter at speed,
comfortable whatever the weather and, largely
because the closed shell is much stiffer than the
open one, it has even better roadholding and
handling capabilities. The car might not be pretty,
but it certainly works.

Bugatti Type 43

Dates built: 1927–31

Introduced in 1927, the Bugatti Type 43 was the world's first 100mph production car. In fact it beat the yardstick very easily, with at least 110mph claimed for any version, and as much as 125mph with factory-tuned engine and higher final drive ratio. It was also flexible enough to start in top gear and accelerate effortlessly to maximum speed. The formula for the 43 was not complicated. Bugatti simply put a mildly detuned version of his supercharged 2.3-litre straight-eight Type 35 GP engine into the underpowered 38 tourer, little modified save for a shorter wheelbase. However, the result was no ill-mannered hot-rod; it was a magnificent car that combined comfort and performance in a way previously undreamed of by all except Bugatti. It was sold with a '3½-seater' Grand Sport body

SPECIFICATIONS	Model Year 1928
Engine type:	**in-line 8-cyl**
Capacity/power:	**2.3 litres/120**
Top speed (mph):	**110**
0–60mph (secs):	**11.7**

and had the classic Bugatti hallmarks of
horseshoe radiator, spoked alloy wheels, cycle
wings and lines very evocative of the smaller GP
racer. It bristled with Bugatti details, from rigid
chassis and exquisite front axle forging to
excellent steering and massive drum brakes.
And from the scream of its supercharger to the
delicate feel of all its controls, it oozes everything
that Bugatti stood for.

Bugatti Type 57SC

Dates built: 1933–40 (Type 57)

The Type 57 survived from 1933 to 1940, but fewer than eighty cars were built and virtually no two were identical. It was the most refined of Bugattis, but also retained the finest Bugatti performance traditions. It was an early project for Bugatti's son Jean, but father Ettore insisted on some traditions, including non-independent front suspension, while Jean contributed the first Bugatti gearbox in unit with the engine. That was a classic straight-eight, originally of 2.9 litres and 120bhp, soon increased to 3.2 litres and 135bhp, with more to come, while the chassis was also improved. In 1936 the 57C was supercharged to deliver 160bhp, and with development reached 200bhp in the 57SC, which had a top speed of more than 110mph. The 57SC combined the sports car model, the 1936 57S, with the blown

SPECIFICATIONS	Model Year 1937
Engine type:	**in-line 8-cyl**
Capacity/power:	**2.9 litres/200bhp**
Top speed (mph):	**110+**
0–60mph (secs):	**10.0**

engine, and became a Bugatti legend. The 57 had many body variations, including saloon, cabriolet, coupé and convertible, but the most famous was the amazing aerodynamic Atlantic coupé, with flowing lines and riveted ridges running the full length of the body and wings. The racing version also won Le Mans in 1937, but, sadly, Jean Bugatti died soon after while testing that car on the public road.

Bugatti EB110 3.5SS

Dates built: 1991–95

In 1991 one of the legendary names of motoring returned to the market, with a car entirely worthy of its famous badge. It was the Bugatti EB110, the 'EB' remembering marque-founder Ettore Bugatti, and the '110' celebrating the 110th anniversary of his birth. There was nothing retro about the car itself though. The EB110 was built around an ultra-modern, carbon-fibre chassis and the distinctly wedge-shaped, slab-sided package was smaller and lighter than almost any other contemporary supercar rival. It had a gloriously high-tech, mid-mounted V12 engine with four camshafts, five valves per cylinder and no fewer than four small turbochargers, for instantaneous responses. All this technology allowed the EB110 to deliver a monstrous 553bhp from its 3.5-litre engine. It

SPECIFICATIONS	Model Year 1994
Engine type:	**V12**
Capacity/power:	**3.5 litres/620bhp**
Top speed (mph):	**220**
0–60mph (secs):	**3.2**

also featured a six-speed gearbox and drive to all four wheels, which is a rarity among supercars. There was also a speed-deployed rear wing to keep the whole package on the ground. And it all worked. The EB110 was not only fast, at 210mph and with 0–60mph in 3.6 seconds, but also beautifully balanced and luxuriously trimmed – with wood, leather and considerable comfort.The 3.5SS was simply an even more extreme EB110, with 620bhp in an even lighter car giving 220mph and 0–60mph in 3.2 seconds. It was a brilliant, much-admired car but, eventually killed in 1995 by various Bugatti company crises, a sadly short-lived one.

1956 Chevrolet Corvette

Dates built: 1956–57

In 1953 the Corvette show car previewed a home-grown rival to the European sports cars that were doing so well in the postwar United States. A glassfibre-bodied two-seater, front-engined and with rear drive, it was small by American standards, European in its styling and simple to the point of being spartan. However, it was the start of a dynasty. It was rushed into production, with plans to tool up very quickly for metal body production, although that never happened and the Corvette still has a plastic body even today.

It was meant to be a sports car but with its original, very dull six-cylinder engine and automatic transmission, its performance was embarrassingly behind its looks and sharp handling, and sales figures were a disaster, so low that the car was almost killed off. But in 1955 it

SPECIFICATIONS	Model Year 1956
Engine type:	**V8**
Capacity/power:	**4.3 litres/225bhp**
Top speed (mph):	**120+**
0–60mph (secs):	**7.5**

was given a second chance with the arrival of V8 muscle and a manual gearbox. In 1956 the package was complete, as the car was wonderfully restyled and the V8 was given even more power. Finally, the Corvette could lay serious claim to being 'America's only true sports car'. The original six had 150bhp, the 1956 V8 had either 210 or 225bhp depending on the version, and this gave the Corvette real performance – at more than 120mph and 0–60mph in 7.5 seconds. From then on there was no looking back.

Chevrolet Corvette ZR-1

Dates built: 1990-95

In 1990 America's favourite sports car gained the power and performance to bring back an edge that had been lost due to US environmental legislation, and turned the Corvette ZR-1 into an all-American supercar. The basic formula stayed the same, with a big V8 engine in the front driving the wheels at the back, all clothed in a shapely glassfibre body like every Corvette from day one, but this was the cleverest 'vette yet. It didn't breach the 'gas-guzzler' taxes thanks to an all-alloy 5.7-litre V8 engine developed by Lotus, the use of clever fuel-saving electronics, and a six-speed manual gearbox as

SPECIFICATIONS	Model Year 1990
Engine type:	**V8**
Capacity/power:	**5.7 litres/375bhp**
Top speed (mph):	**170+**
0–60mph (secs):	**5.5**

standard. With 375bhp it would top 170mph, and could achieve 0–60mph in 5.5 seconds. Thanks to a Performance Handling Package, with computer-controlled Selective Ride Control, traction control and improved power steering, plus wider wheels and tyres and ABS as standard, its road manners were much closer to European preferences than most Corvettes, while it had all the equipment that any comfort-loving owner could ask for, from leather upholstery to air-conditioning. Although all this performance, power and luxury came for a price that was considerably more than an ordinary Corvette, it was still a lot less than any European supercar of similar performance.

1997 Chevrolet Corvette

Dates built: 1997–on

The fifth-generation Corvette, launched in 1997,
retained all the old Corvette traditions but
brought the recipe right up to date. The front-
engine, rear-drive layout, the dramatic glassfibre
two-seater coupé body and the thundering V8
engine were all familiar themes, but the
engineering and detail design all found new levels
of sophistication.

The all-alloy 5.7-litre V8 still had the honest
simplicity of a single camshaft, pushrods and just
two valves per cylinder, but with size on its side it
was able to deliver 344bhp with all the flexibility
for which big American V8s are justly famous.
With a low drag coefficient of only 0.29Cd the
Corvette, with either six-speed manual or four-
speed automatic gearboxes, was now good for
175mph and 0–60mph in less than 5 seconds. It

SPECIFICATIONS	Model Year 1998
Engine type:	**V8**
Capacity/power:	**5.7 litres/344bhp**
Top speed (mph):	**175**
0–60mph (secs):	**4.9**

also handled better than ever, not least because its new, lighter chassis was four times as stiff as that of its predecessor, and the Corvette now had ideal 50/50 weight distribution. It also had wishbone suspension with adjustable damping and composite transverse springs, switchable traction control, run-flat tyres on lightweight magnesium wheels, super-quick power-assisted rack and pinion steering, and massive all-disc brakes with ABS. It all made the latest version of America's favourite sports car the best yet.

DeLorean DMC

Dates built: 1981–82

The DeLorean name became most famous (or infamous) for the company's financial disasters in the 1970s and 1980s, and John Z. DeLorean's arrest on drugs charges in 1982, but in the meantime the DeLorean DMC car had a brief life of its own in the fast lane. It was well-known for its unpainted (and so far as engineering was concerned unnecessary) brushed stainless steel bodywork, which was styled by super-stylist Giugiaro, and for its 'gullwing' doors. It was intended to use a chassis made of an advanced composite material known as ERM, but instead used a backbone chassis with two-piece vacuum-moulded underbody designed by consultants Lotus, who had extensively revamped the original designs. It was rear-engined, powered by a 2.9-litre Renault V6 engine, tuned to give 130bhp for

SPECIFICATIONS	Model Year 1981
Engine type:	**Renault V6**
Capacity/power:	**2.9 litres/130bhp**
Top speed (mph):	**120**
0–60mph (secs):	**10.3**

a top speed of 120mph and 0–62mph in around
10.5 seconds, which was pretty average even
when the car was launched in 1981. Its Lotus-
tweaked handling was reasonably good and
overall it wasn't such a bad car. However, it
wasn't as exciting as the company's dealings and
before long both DMC and company were
history, the company with multi-million-pound
debts, the car with just 5000 sales.

De Tomaso Pantera GT5S

Dates built: 1971– on

In the early 1970s Ford had a winning reputation in motor sport but, surprisingly, the company did not have a big league production sports car of its own. That led them to finance a project by Italian-based Argentinian sports car builder Alessandro de Tomaso to build an affordable supercar that combined great looks with mid-engined technology and, of course, Ford power. The finished product would be sold through Ford's dealer network in the United States and through de Tomaso dealers in Europe, with Ford's support. The Pantera, styled by Ghia and powered by a light, compact Ford V8 engine between driver and racing-style transaxle gearbox, was launched in 1971 – and is still in production today. It had its problems, however. It was a simple design but its build quality was

SPECIFICATIONS	Model Year 1990
Engine type:	**Ford V8**
Capacity/power:	**5.7 litres/350bhp**
Top speed (mph):	**165+**
0–60mph (secs):	**5.4**

never up to mass production standards and Ford
soon distanced themselves from the project, but
the details did improve over the years while the
Pantera never lost its basic appeal – of massive
performance for around half the price of its most
exotic Italian cousins. The fastest of them all, the
GT5S, saw the Pantera into the 1990s with 5.7
litres, around 350bhp, a top speed of 165mph or
more, and 0–60mph in less than 5.5 seconds. And
it still looks terrific.

Dodge Viper GTS

Dates built: 1997–on

The Dodge Viper GTS is among the most
outrageous sports cars in the world. Nothing
about this car is remotely ordinary. The Viper
started as a 1989 show car and became a 1992
production car without losing any of its take-no-
prisoners attitude. In a country obsessed with
political correctness, the open two-seater R/T
burst onto the scene with an 8-litre V10 engine
and 400bhp of thunder under its monstrously
long, wide bonnet. It was only the start. The
roadster grew more powerful and better-
mannered, and alongside it appeared a new
breed of Viper, the GTS. The GTS was a coupé
but it was much more than a Viper with a roof.
Putting on a top made it more comfortable and
civilised (even including wind-up windows and
standard air-conditioning) but crucially for

SPECIFICATIONS	Model Year 1998
Engine type:	**V10**
Capacity/power:	**8.0 litres/455bhp**
Top speed (mph):	**178**
0–60mph (secs):	**5.0**

performance it made the chassis much stiffer and the Viper much more aerodynamic. With power up to 455bhp for all Vipers by this time, the GTS took top speed up by around 20mph to almost 180mph, with 0–60mph in around 5 seconds for a standard car. And there were plenty of tuners who would give a lot more performance than that, beyond 600bhp and towards 200mph.

Duesenberg SJ

Dates built: 1932–37

In the 1930s, the United States was used to cars as spectacular as even the most extreme Duesenberg roadsters, but no one was familiar with the performance that the mighty SJ could offer. In 1935, record breaker Ab Jenkins' SJ-based Mormon Meteor averaged 135.5mph for 24 hours on the Bonneville Salt Flats, and Duesenberg could quote a top-down maximum of 129mph for the production phaeton, with 104mph in second gear and the flexibility to hit 100mph in 20 seconds. The coachbuilt bodies were spectacular, especially the two-seater roadsters with their chromed, flexible exhausts, the chassis were robust but simple, and the power and performance were extraordinary. The huge 6.9-litre twin-cam 32-valve straight-eight, built by Lycoming and introduced in the Model J in 1928,

SPECIFICATIONS	Model Year 1936
Engine type:	**in-line 8-cyl**
Capacity/power:	**6.9 litres/320bhp**
Top speed (mph):	**129**
0–60mph (secs):	**n/a**

was race-bred and gave 265bhp. In 1932 it gained a screaming centrifugal supercharger in the SJ and power leapt to 320bhp, putting the SJ among the fastest cars in the world in the early 1930s and mightily impressive even now. It was also as rare as it was fast. Fewer than 500 Js were built, of which only 36 were SJs, and just two the ultimate short-wheelbase supercharged SSJ.

Facel Vega HK500

Dates built: 1959–61

In 1954 Forges et Ateliers de Construction
d'Eure et de Loire, a company that made machine
tools, aero engine components, office equipment,
kitchen furniture and car bodies, launched its
own car, the Vega. It used a 4.5-litre 180bhp
Chrysler V8 in a drum-braked tubular chassis,
with handsome and beautifully trimmed four-
seater coupé body. It was the first of a line of
prestigious, American-powered, French-styled
Facels that were rare, expensive and always fast.
By 1956 it was badged Facel Vega and in 1959 it
was extensively redesigned as the Facel Vega
HK500. With a 360bhp 6.3-litre Chrysler V8,
it was billed as the world's fastest saloon.
Arguably the two-door coupé was more Grand
Tourer, but, at 140mph and 0–60mph in less than
9 seconds, you couldn't deny the performance,

SPECIFICATIONS	Model Year 1960
Engine type:	**Chrysler V8**
Capacity/power:	**6.3 litres/360bhp**
Top speed (mph):	**140**
0–60mph (secs):	**8.6**

and it had real character. It retained Facel's robust tubular chassis, a choice of manual or automatic transmission, independent front and live-axle rear suspensions, and (before it was very old) all disc brakes. It was luxurious, comfortable, fast, very distinctive and very expensive. Sadly, as the company got into difficulties building a smaller car with their own engines, the HK500 was out of production by 1961.

Ferrari 250GTO

Dates built: 1962–64

To many people the 250GTO is the greatest
Ferrari. Just 39 were built between 1962 and
1964, and it has become one of the most valuable
cars in the world. It is beautiful, designed for
aerodynamic excellence by Giotto Bizzarrini. It is
capable (in 'production' trim) of around 175mph,
and it has an impeccable racing pedigree, winning
the world championship for GT cars three times
in succession from 1962 to 1964. It was Ferrari's
way of bending racing rules, which required at
least 100 of a particular model to be built but
allowed for 'evolution' of an already eligible
model. Ferrari evolved the 250GTO from the
250GT SWB, in his own way. It had a much more
complex chassis and revised rear suspension
(albeit based on the SWB's), that slippery
bodywork, and the engine was set further back

SPECIFICATIONS	Model Year 1964
Engine type:	**V12**
Capacity/power:	**3.0 litres/300bhp**
Top speed (mph):	**175**
0–60mph (secs):	**6.0**

and lower down, with a new five-speed gearbox. The engine was a full-race 3-litre six-carburettor V12, delivering up to 300bhp. The rest of the car was virtually pure racer, with minimal trim, no bumpers, plastic side windows and not even a speedometer. The authorities, after much argument, accepted it as a modified 250GT and gave it the label 'O' for *omologato* (Italian for 'homologation'), for the most famous Ferrari badge of them all.

Ferrari Dino 206GT

Dates built: 1968–69

Dino was Enzo Ferrari's son. He died aged 24, in 1956, and was deeply mourned for the rest of his father's long life. Before he died Dino contributed the philosophy, if not the design, of a V6 engine for Formula 2 racing. In a company famous for its V12s, Dino's name (from Alfredino, or little Alfredo, his real name) became permanently associated with the V6 layout. The jewel-like Dino 206GT was a small car but an immensely important one.

It was the first mid-engined Ferrari road car and the first to sell in larger numbers at a reasonable profit. It helped homologate the compact, lightweight V6 engine for the production-based Formula 2 of the mid-1960s (together with the front-engined Fiat Dino which also used the same Ferrari engine).

SPECIFICATIONS	Model Year 1968
Engine type:	**V6**
Capacity/power:	**2.0 litres/180bhp**
Top speed (mph):	**140+**
0–60mph (secs):	**6.8**

It started with two Pininfarina show cars in 1965 and 1966 and went into production in 1968 as the Dino 206GT. While there was no Ferrari badge on the car, it was one of Ferrari's finest. The 2-litre engine produced 180bhp, giving a top speed of over 140mph and 0–60mph in around 7 seconds, in a car that was small, light and incredibly agile. As it grew into the 246GT, the Dino marked the start of a long line of outstanding smaller Ferraris.

Ferrari 365GTB/4 Daytona

Dates built: 1968–74

In 1968, while others followed the racing fashion of putting the engine behind the driver, Ferrari launched one of the greatest supercars, with its engine in front. The 365GTB/4 Daytona was the pinnacle of his front-engined line, at the time the fastest car in the world, with a top speed of 174mph, 0–60mph in 5.4 seconds, 100mph in only 12.6 seconds – impressive figures even now, astonishing in 1968. The capacity of a single cylinder was 365cc, or in the classic V12 a total of 4.4 litres. GTB was the Gran Turismo Berlinetta

SPECIFICATIONS	Model Year 1973
Engine type:	**V12**
Capacity/power:	**4.4 litres/352bhp**
Top speed (mph):	**174**
0–60mph (secs):	**5.4**

body style, by Pininfarina. The /4 stood for four overhead camshafts. With six twin-choke downdraught Weber carburettors, it produced 352bhp, making the Daytona the most powerful production car of its day, too. With a mainly steel body it was no lightweight, but it had huge flexibility and superb road manners. The all-alloy engine sat well back and the five-speed gearbox was at the rear, for almost perfect weight distribution. Suspension was all double wishbones and coil springs, brakes were all discs and, apart from being rather heavy at low speeds, the Daytona had the grip and balance to challenge any mid-engined rival.

Ferrari 365GT4/BB

Dates built: 1973–76

The letters changed only slightly from the Daytona, but in 1973 Ferrari's philosophy changed considerably. Launching the Pininfarina-styled 365GT4/BB, Ferrari finally joined the ranks of mid-engined supercar makers.

As in the Daytona, engine capacity was once again 365cc per cylinder, with the inevitable dozen cylinders giving a total capacity of 4.4 litres; four was the number of camshafts; and one B stood for the Berlinetta body style. The second B said 'Boxer' for the horizontally opposed flat-12 rather than a more traditional V12. But, as with the engine mid-mounting, this reflected 1970s Ferrari racing designs. The car was predictably controversial. Some saw it as Ferrari catching up with reality, others as breaking with tradition. Few could decide whether it was better or worse

SPECIFICATIONS	Model Year 1973
Engine type:	**flat-12**
Capacity/power:	**4.4 litres/344bhp**
Top speed (mph):	**175**
0–60mph (secs):	**5.5**

than a Daytona. It had 344bhp for a Daytona-like maximum of 175mph, but there the similarity ended. The Berlinetta Boxer wasn't conventional, even for a mid-engined car. The engine sat quite high, with the five-speed gearbox below rather than behind it, to reduce overall length. That was good for packaging, but set the rear weight some way from the ground, so the BB could be interesting on its limits. However, those limits were extremely high and the BB was lighter to drive than the Daytona, and it re-established Ferrari against arch-rival Lamborghini.

Ferrari F40

Dates built: 1987–92

The F40 was named to celebrate Ferrari's fortieth anniversary as a manufacturer, and, with Enzo already in his ninetieth year in 1987 when the F40 was launched, he knew it would be his last great car. It was worthy of its task.

Like his earliest cars it bridged the gap between racing car and road car, and at its launch it was the fastest road car ever built, with a top speed of 201mph, 0–60mph in 3.5 seconds and 0–120mph in just 11.5 seconds. Its only real rival was the Porsche 959, but the F40 was as minimalist as the Porsche was complex. Developed from the earlier 288GTO, it had a mid-mounted V8 of 3 litres with four camshafts, four valves per cylinder and twin turbochargers. Its chassis was a light but massively stiff steel spaceframe reinforced by bonded composite

SPECIFICATIONS	Model Year 1987
Engine type:	**V8**
Capacity/power:	**3.0 litres/478bhp**
Top speed (mph):	**201**
0–60mph (secs):	**3.5**

panels. Its Pininfarina body was mainly of plastics and composites, for light weight, and shaped for maximum aerodynamic stability. The interior was strictly functional, with almost no trim. Only the rear wheels were driven; suspension was race-bred coils and wishbones all round, and brakes were massive ventilated discs of iron sandwiching light alloy for minimum weight. Standing the supercar world on its head, it was a fitting tribute.

Ferrari F50

Dates built: 1995–97

In 1995, eight years after the F40, Ferrari launched the F50, a car widely described as the closest thing to experiencing an F1 car on the road. It was limited to a run of just 349, each with a £329,000 price tag, and reserved for Ferrari's most prized customers. Unlike almost any other major-league supercar, it was an open two-seater, its shape owing more to aerodynamics than to aesthetics. Behind the cockpit, instead of a turbocharged V8 like the F40's, it had a cousin of Ferrari's 1990 GP-winning V12. The race engine's pneumatic valve gear was replaced with conventional springs, and the ultimate edge of GP tuning sacrificed for drivability and durability. However, by increasing capacity from 3.5 to 4.7 litres, Ferrari conjured up 520bhp, with a character all its own. With a maximum of

SPECIFICATIONS	Model Year 1996
Engine type:	**V12**
Capacity/power:	**4.7 litres/520bhp**
Top speed (mph):	**202**
0–60mph (secs):	**3.7**

202mph and 0–60mph in 3.7 seconds, it isn't much faster than an F40 and is slower than a McLaren, but the delivery is unique. Like the F40, the interior is purely functional, but the F50 is even more responsive and immediate. It sounds like a racing car, vibrates like a racing car, responds to every input and steers and stops like a racing car. Exactly as Ferrari intended.

Ferrari 550 Maranello

Dates built: 1996–on

In 1996, not for the first time, Ferrari defied convention. Late into mid-engines in the mid-1960s, Ferrari now opted out, for two of their largest and most powerful models – re-inventing the ultimate front-engined GT car. In 1993 came the 456GT, Ferrari's first front-engined GT since the Daytona and universally received as a brilliant step forward. Then in 1996 came the 550 Maranello, a two-seater where the 456 was a 2+2, even more compact, lighter, more powerful, faster and right at the top of the range. Its engine is an upgraded version of the 456's four-cam 48-valve V12, with lighter internal components and special inlet and exhaust

SPECIFICATIONS	Model Year 1997
Engine type:	**V12**
Capacity/power:	**5.5 litres/485bhp**
Top speed (mph):	**199**
0–60mph (secs):	**4.5**

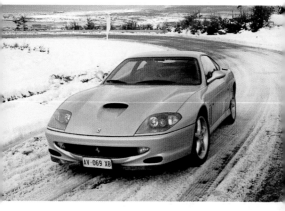

systems. Capacity is 5.5 litres, power output
485bhp, through a six-speed manual transaxle,
rear-mounted for optimum weight distribution.
The chassis and shell use exotic steel and
aluminium sandwich materials for maximum
stiffness with minimum weight, suspension has
electronically controlled variable damping and
the huge wheels are magnesium, all to help
handling. The 550 Maranello has luxury, great
comfort, few vices and massive performance. Not
only does 0–60mph occupy just 4.5 seconds and
0–100 a mere 10.2, but the top speed is 199mph.

Ferrari 360 Modena

Dates built: 1999–on

The 360 Modena, launched in 1999 as successor to the hugely successful F355, was another in the new generation of user-friendly Ferraris, like the 456 and the 550. It was faster and arguably better in almost every respect than its much-loved predecessor. Styled by Pininfarina, the sleekly aerodynamic coupé looked stunning. The quest for lightness combined with strength led to an aluminium spaceframe construction, so although it was slightly bigger than the F355, it was some 200lb lighter. The mid-mounted 40-valve V8 was stretched to 3.6 litres and a full 400bhp, with

SPECIFICATIONS	Model Year 1999
Engine type:	**V8**
Capacity/power:	**3.6 litres/400bhp**
Top speed (mph):	**185**
0–60mph (secs):	**4.3**

improved mid-range torque. The six-speed manual transmission had the option of F1-style sequential semi-automatic paddle shifts, the brakes were hugely powerful and communicative, and the steering razor-sharp and alive. There was traction control if you wanted it to rein in the 185mph, 0–60mph in 4.3 seconds performance, but the downforce-generating underbody shape and all-wishbone suspension with adaptive damping did a pretty good job anyway, and the 360 Modena had exceptional body control – even a fairly forgiving nature when you approached its limits. However, most of all it had the Ferrari sound, and there's nothing in the world like it.

Fiat Coupé 20v turbo

Dates built: 1996–on

In 1994 Fiat launched a quirkily styled two-door
2+2 coupé that was a flier, even with its original
normally aspirated and turbocharged four-
cylinder engines – the latter derived from the
rally-bred Lancia Integrale. In 1996 the fours
were replaced by new five-cylinder 20-valve
engines that were more refined, easier to drive
and more economical. They were also more
powerful. In turbo form, the Coupé became
the fastest front-wheel-drive car in the world,
achieving a maximum speed of almost 150mph
and 0–60mph in 6 seconds dead. The extra
25bhp, making 220bhp, turned the Coupé into a
junior league supercar, backed by fast responses,
a slick five-speed gearbox and enough mid-range
flexibility to make the compact Fiat a real rocket
in everyday driving conditions. It also had a very

SPECIFICATIONS	Model Year 1998
Engine type:	**in-line 5-cyl**
Capacity/power:	**2.0 litres/220bhp**
Top speed (mph):	**148**
0–60mph (secs):	**6.0**

competent chassis, updated with tauter suspension, and super-quick steering borrowed from its cousin the Alfa GTV. Its brakes were upgraded to match the new performance, adopting large ventilated front and solid rear discs, with Brembo four-pot calipers all round. And it was special not only because it was the fastest front-drive production car, but also because it offered so much performance for its price. In fact it was unique.

Ford GT40

Dates built: 1963–67

The GT40 was Ford's challenge to Ferrari. In
the early 1960s, Ford promoted a new sporting
image under the headline Total Performance,
encompassing everything from saloon cars to
F1 and Indianapolis. Pursuing an ambition to
win Le Mans, Ford even tried to buy Ferrari
and, having failed to do so, set out to beat them
instead. The result was the GT40, primarily a
racing car but also a road car to rival the greatest.
It started with Ford taking a mid-engined Lola
racer, and in just 10 months turning it into
the first GT40. It looked stunning, and the
40 famously referred to its standing only 40
inches tall. It also had the same compact and
lightweight Ford 289 V8 that appeared in the
Cobra, and, with up to 400bhp on tap and superb
aerodynamics, it would nudge 200mph in racing

SPECIFICATIONS	Model Year 1964
Engine type:	**V8**
Capacity/power:	**4.7 litres/400bhp**
Top speed (mph):	**200**
0–60mph (secs):	**4.3**

trim. It took three years to do it, but after overcoming early stability and reliability problems it did win Le Mans, and it became a remarkable commercial success. More than 130 GT40s were sold in various guises, including the roadgoing GT40P. Detuned to 335bhp, with softer suspension, silencers and a well-trimmed cabin, it was still a 165mph car and indisputably a winner.

Ford Mustang GT350

Dates built: 1965–69

The Ford Mustang, launched in 1964, was the original pony-car – it was a practical, all-American automobile, but more of a sports car than most Americans had ever thought they would buy. Aggressively priced and fast-selling, the Mustang changed Ford's image from conservative to racy. It was a four-seater car cleverly styled to look like a rakish two-seater and came with such a huge list of options that owners could specify anything from an economical runabout to a firebreathing dragster. It was available in notchback, fastback or convertible bodies. At its launch there was a choice of two relatively modest straight-six or V8 engines, but as time went on the choice widened, and by 1968 it was possible to specify the legendary 427cu in V8, with 390bhp. The GT350 was a Mustang

SPECIFICATIONS   Model Year 1965

Engine type:	**V8**
Capacity/power:	**4.7 litres/306bhp**
Top speed (mph):	**125**
0–60mph (secs):	**4.5**

classic, contrived with the help of Carroll Shelby and based on the good-looking GT 2+2 fastback. Shelby created the 350GT in 1965, for racing but also as a special production model. The first ones were the best, before the stylists and marketing men made it heavier and softer. It had the lightweight 4.7-litre 289 V8 engine used in the Mustang and Cobra, tuned by Shelby to deliver 306 rather than 271bhp and mated to a sporty four-speed manual transmission. It would hit 125mph and 0–60mph in 6.8 seconds, and Shelby made it handle and stop beautifully, too. If you want to remember how, just watch Steve McQueen in *Bullitt*.

Ford RS200

Dates built: 1984–86

The RS200 was Ford's challenger in the Group B
rally arena, and perhaps the most extreme
'production' Ford of them all. Production in this
case was a strictly relative term. Almost nothing
was taken from the production-line parts bin,
and the term really meant just enough cars to
satisfy the rallying rules, but you actually could
buy one in road trim – if you didn't mind a few
rough edges. The RS200 was not a refined car.
It was quite comfortable but it was also noisy,
mechanically harsh and demanding to drive –
hardly surprisingly because it was at heart a
competition car. It saw Ford experimenting for
the first time with four-wheel drive for rallying,
and its enormously sophisticated composite-and-
alloy chassis was designed by Grand Prix and
sports racing car designer Tony Southgate. Its

SPECIFICATIONS	Model Year 1986
Engine type:	**in-line 4-cyl**
Capacity/power:	**2.0 litres/250bhp**
Top speed (mph):	**154**
0–60mph (secs):	**6.1**

body was the work of Ford styling house Ghia, with aerodynamics by Ford's Motorsport division. The mid-mounted 2-litre engine was turbocharged and produced at least 250bhp in 'off-the-shelf' trim, which was good for 150mph and 0–60mph in 4.5 seconds. At least 340bhp was possible with a simple engine management change, and for competition even more than that, making the RS200 a very fast Ford.

Ford Sierra Cosworth RS500

Dates built: 1986-1993

In the 1980s, Ford redefined the high-performance version of the family saloon, with the Sierra RS Cosworth – a car to follow in the wheeltracks of the Lotus Cortina, the Escort RS and the rapid V6 Capris. They all started life as road cars but always had a role as race and rally cars, once enough had been sold to make them eligible. As a result, they offered a lot of performance for price, and none more so than the Sierras. Cosworth was well known for its Ford-financed racing engines, including the DFV F1 engine, and in mid-1983 Ford saw a racing engine

SPECIFICATIONS	Model Year 1987
Engine type:	**in-line 4-cyl**
Capacity/power:	**2.0 litres/224bhp**
Top speed (mph):	**153**
0–60mph (secs):	**6.2**

Cosworth was developing for the Sierra, and the story began. The engine was a 2-litre twin-cam 16-valve turbo, and in 1986 it went into production in the stiff shell of the two-door two-window Sierra. With 204bhp, it offered 150mph for less money than any other competitor. The RS500 was the first-evolution version, specifically aimed at competition, which required 500 examples to be built. With a bigger turbo and other modifications, power increased to 224bhp (or over 400 in race trim), top speed went up to 153mph and 0–60mph fell to 6.2 seconds.

Frazer Nash Le Mans Replica

Dates built: 1948–1953

Frazer Nash was a small British company that made sporty cars in tiny numbers and often managed giant-killing racing performances. At first it was famous for its chain-drive models; later it had strong associations with BMW, making what were in effect British versions of BMW's pre-war sports cars; after the war it started building sports cars with BMW-designed engines built by fellow car-maker Bristol. Between 1948 and 1953 the Le Mans Replica was an off-the-shelf racer that could double as a very fast road car. Its family tree ran from the Roadster, based on the pre-war BMW Mille Miglia racer, to the High Speed and the Competition – and when one finished third at Le Mans in 1949, subsequent cars became Le Mans Replicas. They were hand-

SPECIFICATIONS	Model Year 1952
Engine type:	**Bristol in-line 6-cyl**
Capacity/power:	**2.0 litres/141bhp**
Top speed (mph):	**115**
0–60mph (secs):	**7.9**

built, with a strong tubular ladder chassis, transverse-leaf front suspension and Frazer Nash's own torsion-bar rear suspension. With around 141bhp from its snarling six-cylinder Bristol engine, a typical Le Mans Replica would do 115mph and 0–60mph in 7.9 seconds. It wasn't easy to drive on the limit, but it still has the handling to run rings round cars half its age.

Honda S800

Dates built: 1965–70

Having stood the motorcycle world on its ears, Honda turned its attention to four wheels, and in 1965 they launched their first sports car into Europe, the amazing S800. Amazing because its engine was so tiny, even when compared to small European cars like the Sprite and Midget. However, what it lacked in size, it made up for with technology. It came as either coupé or convertible, both with that jewel of a twin-cam four-carburettor engine – only 791cc but so free-revving and free-breathing

SPECIFICATIONS	Model Year 1965
Engine type:	**in-line 4-cyl**
Capacity/power:	**791cc/70bhp**
Top speed (mph):	**96**
0–60mph (secs):	**12.7**

that it produced 70bhp, giving 0–60mph in less than 13 seconds. The gearbox was an all-synchromesh four-speed manual, brakes were front discs and rear drums, suspension wishbone and torsion bar at the front, live axle and coil springs at the rear, and steering was by rack and pinion. The S800 was as special to drive as its specification suggests. It was well equipped, nicely trimmed, very well made and usually remarkably reliable. It was also pretty quick for such a tiny car, not so much in top speed but for its amazing eagerness to rev and its ability to attack any twisty road with huge enthusiasm, if only marginal brakes. But oh, that engine!

Honda NSX

Dates built: 1990–on

The NSX, introduced in 1990, is one of the most civilised supercars in the world. It is capable of around 170mph and 0–60mph in 5.3 seconds, but it is also comfortable enough to go long-distance touring and docile enough to potter around town with the shopping. Where its European rivals almost all have some sort of raw edges, the NSX is smooth and entirely untemperamental. It started life with the classic mid-engined layout and a 3-litre 270bhp four-cam V6, which later grew to 3.2 litres and 276bhp. That is the heart of the car: a fantastic engine that pulls like a train and goes from near silent cruise to spine-tingling howl at the press of the throttle. There's now a choice of manual or automatic transmissions, and coupé or targa bodywork, but the basics remain the same. The chassis is quite exceptional, with

SPECIFICATIONS	Model Year 1995
Engine type:	**V6**
Capacity/power:	**3.0 litres/270bhp**
Top speed (mph):	**170**
0–60mph (secs):	**5.3**

lightweight aluminium suspension components contributing to massive grip with perfectly controlled responses, and, since the NSX gained power steering, a light but precise controllability. It has Honda's typically excellent build quality, and the most frequent criticisms are that it looks slightly ungainly and isn't supercar special inside – but the driving experience is sensational.

Iso Grifo

Dates built: 1965–74

With the profits he made from building the Isetta bubble car in the fuel-starved 1950s, Italian industrialist Renzo Rivolta went on to develop a very different type of car: the fast and brutal Iso Grifo. Built between 1965 and 1974, it was another example of that classic formula: big, affordable American horses housed in a state-of-the-art European chassis, and in this case clothed in wonderfully aggressive Italian styling.

Like his earlier Iso-Rivolta 2+2 of 1962, the Iso Grifo was engineered by the man also famously responsible for the Ferrari 250GTO, Giotto Bizzarrini. It was styled by Giugiaro, built by Bertone with a steel shell welded to a pressed steel chassis, and powered by Chevrolet – in this case, in the guise of a lightly stressed 5.4-litre V8 taken from the Corvette. That produced 365bhp,

SPECIFICATIONS	Model Year 1970
Engine type:	**Chevrolet V8**
Capacity/power:	**5.4 litres/365bhp**
Top speed (mph):	**170**
0–60mph (secs):	**6.0**

but you could have more if you so desired, from a
7-litre Ford V8. The Grifo was low, wide,
handsome and fast – at up to 170mph with
0–60mph in 6 seconds for the quickest versions.
It was well built, luxuriously trimmed and
equipped, and it handled and stopped with the
best of them. Sadly, for some people, the fact that
it had American horses under the long bonnet
rather than thoroughbred Italian ones counted
against it, but these people didn't know what they
were missing.

Jaguar XKSS

Dates built: 1957

In the 1950s road cars often turned into racing cars, and racers occasionally turned into road cars – which is how the Le Mans-winning Jaguar D-Type became the XKSS.

The D-Type, created in 1954 to win Le Mans, was a technical masterpiece. Jaguar had won Le Mans in 1951 and 1953 with the C-Type; to win the race again they needed a car that was lighter, more powerful and more aerodynamic. To achieve this the D-Type was built around aircraft principles. Instead of the tubular chassis that was used in the C-Type, it used a riveted alloy monocoque tub with tubular front and rear subframes carrying engine and suspension. The engine was the 3.4-litre triple-carburettor twin-cam straight-six, suspension was by torsion bars, there were disc brakes all round and the D-Type

SPECIFICATIONS	Model Year 1957
Engine type:	**in-line 6-cyl**
Capacity/power:	**3.4 litres/250bhp**
Top speed (mph):	**150**
0–60mph (secs):	**5.2**

was shaped in the wind tunnel by aerodynamicist
Malcolm Sayer. It won Le Mans three times, in
1955, 1956 and 1957, and countless other races.

Customer D-Types were occasionally seen
on the road, but in 1957 Jaguar produced just 16
wonderous examples of the real road car, the
XKSS. It did have a silencer, windscreen, folding
soft-top and passenger door, but underneath it
was pure D-type: 250bhp, 150mph, 0–60mph in
5.2 seconds and all.

Jaguar XK150

Dates built: 1957–61

There were two things that defined Jaguar's sports cars through the 1950s and 1960s: that racing improved the breed and that they achieved this with very little money. The first of the 1950s racing cars, the C-Type, was derived from a road car, the XK 120, and the 120 also started the line that led to the magnificent XK150. The XK120 was the sensation of the 1948 Motor Show as a beautiful two-seater roadster, and a planned run of 200 aluminium-bodied cars gave way to full production of steel-bodied cars and the family that followed.

The XK120 had a 3.4-litre twin-cam six-cylinder engine that produced 160bhp; the XK150S arrived in 1957 and, between 1958 and 1961, raised the stakes to 3.8 litres and 265bhp. The 120 and 150 figures refer to Jaguar's claimed

SPECIFICATIONS	Model Year 1958
Engine type:	**in-line 6-cyl**
Capacity/power:	**3.8 litres/265bhp**
Top speed (mph):	**150**
0–60mph (secs):	**7.0**

maximum speeds for the cars, and as prepared and run by the factory they would certainly do those figures. The 150 would also dispatch 0–60 mph in around 7 seconds, which was truly exceptional for the late 1950s. On the downside, by the time the XK150 had fully evolved, the XK chassis was starting to show its age, given it was now 10 years old, and further development (including the first disc brakes) couldn't quite make up for a dating design.

Jaguar MkII

Dates built: 1955–69

Perhaps the most telling measure of the performance potential of the Jaguar MkII saloon is that for a while in the 1960s it was the getaway car of choice for robbers, and chase car of choice for the police. It was another archetypal Jaguar, offering bafflingly good style, luxury and performance for a remarkable price, and it was one of the greatest ever performance saloons. It had many of the genes of Jaguar's sports cars, including a choice of six-cylinder engines from 2.4 to 3.8 litres, the biggest and most powerful with 220bhp and a top speed of 125mph, which would frighten many a sports car in the MkII's day. Launched in 1955, the 2.4 was Jaguar's first unit construction saloon, and, when the 3.4 and 3.8 MkIIs added power to the style, the 'small' Jaguar became one of the most desirable cars in

SPECIFICATIONS	Model Year 1960
Engine type:	**in-line 6-cyl**
Capacity/power:	**3.8 litres/220bhp**
Top speed (mph):	**125**
0–60mph (secs):	**8.5**

the world. It had everything: speed, wood and leather cabin luxury, exceptional comfort and sporting looks – especially with the optional wire wheels. It built an enviable reputation in racing, particularly with the Coombs 3.8 versions, and (latterly as the simpler 240 and 340) it survived until 1969, but long after production ceased it is still a Jaguar icon.

Jaguar E-Type

Dates built: 1961–71

The E-Type, launched in March 1961, was another Jaguar sensation. It was stunningly beautiful, with performance to shame cars of twice the price. It was a descendant of the Le Mans-winning D-Type and its roadgoing clone the XKSS, but it was designed for mass production on a Jaguar budget. It relied on sound basic engineering, refined by racing and with maximum style and minimum non-functional frills. Like the D-Type, it was designed by the brilliant aerodynamicist Malcolm Sayer around a monocoque centre section with tubular front and rear subframes carrying engine and suspension. The latter was now all-independent, giving excellent ride and handling; the former was the classic 3.8 twin-cam six, following on from the XK150. With three SU carburettors it gave

SPECIFICATIONS	Model Year 1961
Engine type:	**in-line 6-cyl**
Capacity/power:	**3.8 litres/265bhp**
Top speed (mph):	**150+**
0–60mph (secs):	**6.9**

265bhp, with great reliability and a smooth, docile temperament. The sensational E-Type was as fast as it looked, with a top speed of over 150mph and 0–60mph in under 7 seconds. The first were the best. In 1964 it got the 4.2 engine but it was never as quick because more trim had added weight. The later 2+2s and V12s were slower again, but the E-Type's reputation was already secure.

Jaguar XJ220

Dates built: 1992–94

In the late 1990s, you still couldn't buy more performance for your money than you could with a Jaguar, because the incredible XJ220 had become one of the supercar bargains of the century. In the 1980s, prior to production, even well-heeled customers were requested to place deposits to buy the car, as the total price topped a staggering £1 million. But by the end of the century it could be bought for barely a tenth of that figure and although the XJ220 had first appeared in 1992, the magic of the car remained. Speeds of 220mph, and 60mph in 3.7 seconds, still put it at the sharp end of the supercar scale, and were even more impressive in a car with the physical presence of the big Jag. For all its size, it was a wonderfully attractive car, which was luxuriously trimmed and had enough room to

SPECIFICATIONS	Model Year 1992
Engine type:	**V6**
Capacity/power:	**3.5 litres/542bhp**
Top speed (mph):	**220**
0–60mph (secs):	**3.7**

make any driver comfortable. It had a twin-turbo 3.5-litre V6 engine delivering 542bhp through the rear wheels, after Jaguar ditched plans for four-wheel drive and sophisticated electronic suspension controls very early on in production. Suspension was finalised as being by race-bred wishbones all round. There were also brake discs the size of dustbin lids, and wheels and tyres that would not have been out of place on a racetrack. Added to this it also had the comfort for which Jaguar has always been renowned, and a more practical and forgiving nature than seems possible in such a high-performance car. Again, the question is how did they do it?

Jensen Interceptor FF

Dates built: 1967–71

Jensens had style – large, luxurious, lazy sports tourers, latterly using off-the-shelf American V8 power. They weren't afraid of innovation either. At the 1965 Motor Show Jensen displayed their controversially styled C-V8 with two very exotic features. The car had four-wheel drive and was badged C-V8 FF, for Ferguson Formula, after four-wheel-drive designer Harry Ferguson, and it adopted a Dunlop Maxaret aircraft anti-lock brake system. It was a prototype; a year later Jensen introduced the sharp-edged and modern Touring-styled Interceptor, a two-door coupé including another FF model, now destined for production. The robust steel chassis, 6.3-litre 325bhp Chrysler V8 and three-speed Torqueflite automatic transmission, disc brakes and luxurious trim were all familiar; the four-wheel drive and

SPECIFICATIONS	Model Year 1967
Engine type:	**Chrysler V8**
Capacity/power:	**6.3 litres/325bhp**
Top speed (mph):	**135**
0–60mph (secs):	**7.0**

anti-skid braking were revolutionary for a
production sports car, but it all worked well
and, when it went into production in 1967, the
135mph FF was well received. Unfortunately it
didn't last. The Interceptor grew more powerful
and faster with the 7.2-litre SP in 1971, but at
the expense of the FF, which was dropped in
December, a victim of its own complexity after
just 320 had been built.

Lamborghini 400GT

Dates built: 1966–68

When tractor-maker Ferruccio Lamborghini decided to challenge Ferrari's crown, he did it with style. In 1963 Lamborghini founded his company and set up a factory; and in the same year he showed his first car, as a prototype at the Turin Show. The car had a controversially styled 2+2 body, and a sensational new all-Lamborghini V12 engine, which was mated to a five-speed manual gearbox in the front of an all-independently-sprung, all-disc-braked, rear-drive chassis. It succeeded in launching Lamborghini straight into Ferrari territory. In 1964 the car went into production as the 350GT, elegantly restyled by Touring, with the 3.5-litre V12 toned down slightly from its rabid prototype specification, but still with 280bhp to give the newcomer a top speed of more than 150mph in a

SPECIFICATIONS	Model Year 1966
Engine type:	**V12**
Capacity/power:	**4.0 litres/320bhp**
Top speed (mph):	**158**
0–60mph (secs):	**6.9**

car that also handled brilliantly and now looked wonderful too. In 1966 it was joined by a close relation, the 400GT, subtly restyled with four headlamps and, more significantly, with engine capacity up to 4 litres, power to 320bhp, top speed to almost 160mph and 0–60mph down below 7 seconds. The 400GT stayed in production until 1968, and confirmed that Lamborghini was serious, but it was only the merest hint of just how serious.

Lamborghini Miura SV

Dates built: 1966–73

At the 1965 Geneva Show, alongside the
latest 400GT coupé, Lamborghini showed a
remarkable unclothed chassis. The platform was
pressed steel with a fabricated cradle for engine
and suspension, all extensively perforated for
lightness. Behind the low but wide two-seater
cockpit sat the 4-litre Lamborghini V12,
transversely mounted with the five-speed gearbox
and final drive cleverly integrated into a modified
crankcase – rather like a huge Mini. Most people
thought it was a racing prototype, until a year
later when it reappeared, clothed in a stunning
body styled by Marcello Gandini at Bertone, as
the production Miura. It was Lamborghini's first
mid-engined supercar, beating Ferrari to the
genre by some eight years. It was a well-trimmed,
well-equipped car and it had all the performance

SPECIFICATIONS	Model Year 1971
Engine type:	**V12**
Capacity/power:	**4.0 litres/385bhp**
Top speed (mph):	**170+**
0–60mph (secs):	**5.9**

in the world. With coil and wishbone suspension
all round, it had a supple ride and fine
roadholding, although it was nerve-testing around
its very high limits. As the P400 it started with
350bhp and grew, with matching chassis and
aerodynamic improvements, through the 370bhp
S of 1969 to the ultimate Miura, the 385bhp
SV of 1971, which could exceed 170mph, with
0–60mph in under 6 seconds and 100mph
in 14 seconds.

Lamborghini Countach qv

Dates built: 1974–91

In Lamborghini's local dialect, 'Countach!' is an expression of amazement, and Nuccio Bertone uttered it when he saw Marcello Gandini's Lamborghini prototype in 1971. The name stuck and Countach went into production in 1974, another stunning Lamborghini supercar. Sharper lines replaced the Miura's curves and the designation LP400 said the mid-engine was no longer transverse but *Longitudinale Posteriore*. To accommodate it, the five-speed gearbox was ahead of the 4-litre 375bhp V12 and the final drive behind it, linked by a shaft through the engine. It was a brilliant solution from engineer Paolo Stanzani, making Countach better balanced and more reliable than the complex Miura, and more compact. Over the years it grew ever more aggressive visually, with wider wheels and more

SPECIFICATIONS	Model Year 1985
Engine type:	**V12**
Capacity/power:	**5.2 litres/455bhp**
Top speed (mph):	**180**
0–60mph (secs):	**3.6**

extreme aerodynamics, and mechanically, as power continued to grow. In 1978, with Pirelli P7 low-profile tyres, it became the LP400S, and soon after gained a 4.8-litre V12 as the LP500S, which was cleaner but no more powerful. In 1985 more power arrived, as Lamborghini launched the Countach qv quattrovalvole, with 5.2 litres, four valves per cylinder and 455bhp, for a maximum of around 180mph and 0–60mph in 3.6 seconds. Once again, Lamborghini had thrown down the gauntlet to Ferrari.

Lamborghini LM002

Dates built: 1982–90

Lamborghinis were rarely like other supercars, and Lamborghini's LM002 was not even like other Lamborghinis. Lambos like the Miura, the Countach and the Diablo were sexily smooth and aerodynamic. However, in the aerodynamic stakes, the LM002 was at the opposite end of the scale, being the size of a small house and almost as square and chunky. It measured more than 6 feet from ground to roofline, it was more than 16 feet long on a huge wheelbase of 9 feet 10 inches, and it was over six-and-a-half feet wide. It had around a foot of ground clearance and it weighed well over two-and-a-half tons dry, or nearly three-and-a-half fully loaded.

However, it was still a real Lamborghini, a Lamborghini off-roader. It wasn't designed for

SPECIFICATIONS	Model Year 1986
Engine type:	**V12**
Capacity/power:	**5.2 litres/450bhp**
Top speed (mph):	**125**
0–60mph (secs):	**8.5**

country lanes so much as for wide open plains and deserts, and under the massive bonnet was the Countach's 5.2-litre V12 engine, delivering 450bhp via all four 11-inch-wide wheels and their huge Kevlar-reinforced 345/60VR17 tyres. That was enough power to hurl all that weight to 60mph in just 8.5 seconds and on to around 125mph alternativly select the lowest of the ten forward gears and it could climb almost vertical gradients. No, not an average Lamborghini.

Lamborghini Diablo SV

Dates built: 1991–on

After
Miura and
Countach
rewrote the
supercar
rules
through

the 1960s, 1970s and 1980s, the Diablo has
upheld the tradition through the 1990s, as one of
the longest-lived supercars of all, and still one of
the fastest. It is son-of-Countach, with many
lessons learned. It was again styled by Gandini,
and retains the scissor doors and wide, wedge
stance, with the long tail accommodating the
V12 engine behind the gearbox in familiar style.
It has grown more powerful, more technically
sophisticated and, of course, faster. Diablos come

SPECIFICATIONS	Model Year 1999
Engine type:	**V12**
Capacity/power:	**5.7 litres/530bhp**
Top speed (mph):	**200**
0–60mph (secs):	**3.8**

in several forms, including a Roadster with lift-out roof panels, and four-wheel drive in the Diablo VT, which is reassuring when the going gets slippery. The purest Diablo of all is the simplest: the lightweight, two-wheel-drive Diablo SV, which was based on the SV-R race car. Like the rest of the series, it uses the all-alloy 5.7-litre four-cam, 48-valve V12 engine, uprated in 1999 to give 530bhp and more flexibility than ever before. Being 95kg lighter than its siblings, it is geared for maximum acceleration, including 0–60mph in 3.8 seconds, and a top speed of exactly 200mph, which is 9mph short of the others but comes up even more quickly.

Lancia Stratos

Dates built: 1972–75

As a competition car, the Stratos heralded a new era of high-tech rallying; the road car made the rally cars possible. It was one of the first 'homologation specials', built in just sufficient numbers for 'production' competition regulations. It began with two futuristic Lancia-powered Bertone show cars, the Stratos in 1970 and Stratos HF in 1971, looking very like the production car. The rally car debuted in 1972; by late 1974, Bertone had built 500 cars, enough to qualify for full homologation. The Stratos won successive world championships from 1974 to 1976 and rounded off a glorious career by winning the Monte Carlo Rally in 1979, while the road version became a legend.

The amazing looks speak for themselves; underneath was a thinly disguised racing car. The

SPECIFICATIONS	Model Year 1974
Engine type:	**Ferrari Dino V6**
Capacity/power:	**2.0 litres/190bhp**
Top speed (mph):	**140**
0–60mph (secs):	**6.8**

chassis was a monocoque centre section with tubular extensions at the front. At the rear a cage contained the transverse engine, mid-mounted and made by Ferrari, the 2-litre Dino V6 with 190bhp for the road, up to 290bhp for the rally cars. Roadgoing top speed was 140mph with 0–60mph in 6.8 seconds, but the most spectacular thing about the Stratos was its incredibly agile handling, born of the ultra-short wheelbase, the mid-engine – and the fact that this really was a rally car on the road.

Lancia Delta Integrale

Dates built: 1988–93

Like its stablemate the Stratos, the Delta Integrale was a homologation special, and like the Stratos the competition Integrale won its quota of world rally championships. Unlike the Stratos, however, the Integrale was based on a car that already existed, the relatively humble Delta. There was nothing humble about the Integrale, though. The first version appeared in 1988, hot on the heels of the front-drive Delta HF Turbo and the HF 4WD that had dominated the 1987 world rally championship. That first production Integrale had an 8-valve 2-litre four-pot turbo engine, 185bhp, four-wheel drive, and aggressive new bodywork with flared arches and sideskirts. In true rally car form it then evolved, getting lighter and more powerful. A 16-valve engine took power up to 200bhp,

SPECIFICATIONS	Model Year 1991
Engine type:	**in-line 4-cyl**
Capacity/power:	**2.0 litres/200bhp**
Top speed (mph):	**137**
0–60mph (secs):	**5.5**

which was pretty hefty in a compact five-door hatchback, even with four-wheel drive, and top speed went up from 113 to 137mph while 0–60mph times fell from 6.2 to 5.5 seconds, and the final HE evolution was even quicker. The real joy of the Integrale, though, was – and still is – in its huge grip and stunningly sharp handling, steering and brakes. That's what made it almost every road tester's favourite.

Light Car Company Rocket

Dates built: 1992–on

The Rocket was not like other supercars.
Designed and built by former racing driver Chris
Craft and Grand Prix designer Gordon Murray,
the Rocket aimed to recreate the feel of a single-
seater racing car for the road. And it did – even
with a tiny second seat behind the driver. It had
a complex spaceframe chassis, naked in the snug
cockpit, it had motorcycle instruments, exposed
wheels hung on coil with wishbone suspension
and shrouded in carbonfibre mudguards, and it
had bodywork resembling a 1950s GP car. It had
a Japanese motorcycle engine behind the cockpit
– a liquid-cooled 1-litre twin-cam 20-valve four-
carburettor four-cylinder from the Yamaha
FZR1000. Its 143bhp in a car weighing only
775lb gave a power-to-weight ratio to match an
F40. To cope with a relative lack of torque and

SPECIFICATIONS	Model Year 1993
Engine type:	**Yamaha in-line 4-cyl**
Capacity/power:	**1 litres/143bhp**
Top speed (mph):	**130+**
0–60mph (secs):	**4.5**

screaming rev band, it had a five-speed gearbox and special transaxle, allowing high and low final drive ratios, and reverse gear. It drove as it looked, like a racing car on the road, claiming a top speed of over 130mph and 0–60mph times under 5 seconds. It even sounded like a racing car, and an F1 car at that.

Lotus/Caterham Seven

Dates built: 1957–on

It's the longest-lived fast car in the business, among the most imitated and the least complicated. It arrived in 1957 as a Lotus and, when Lotus thought its day was done, Caterham acquired the manufacturing rights . That was 1973 and they're still building the amazing Lotus/Caterham Seven. It was designed by Colin Chapman, to be sold in either fully assembled or tax-exempt build-it-yourself component form. Its philosophy was simple – minimum weight, a race-style chassis plus ample power equal one of the most exciting sports cars in the world. In detail the recipe has changed but the taste is the same. The Seven's steering, brakes, roadholding and handling are close to a racing car's. In 1957 a 1.2-litre Ford sidevalve engine and three-speed

SPECIFICATIONS Model Year 1999

Engine type:	**in-line 4-cyl**
Capacity/power:	**1.8 litres/190bhp** (Superlight R)
Top speed (mph):	**140**
0–60mph (secs):	**4**

gearbox were the starting point but, as the
spaceframe-chassised, alloy-bodied Seven
weighed barely half a ton, even that was quick. In
1999, while looking little different save for wider
wheels, the Seven Superlight, at 470kg with
133bhp and six gears, is the testers' practical
favourite. The Superlight R has even more power
and the GM-engined 2-litre 175bhp Super Seven
HPC nudges 5 seconds for 60mph. No wonder
they call it a four-wheeled motorbike.

Lotus Elan

Dates built: 1962–74

The Lotus Elan was another masterpiece from Colin Chapman. It was a tiny and apparently simple vehicle, but bristled with the brilliant engineering touches that marked Chapman out as a car designer of true genius. In 1962 the Elan replaced the Elite coupé and, as an open car, demanded a separate chassis instead of the Elite's innovative but troublesome glassfibre monocoque. Accordingly, Chapman designed a very strong, deep steel backbone, forked at either end to carry engine and suspension, and clothed it in a beautifully simple glassfibre body with pop-up headlamps. The engine used for the Elan was another big leap for Lotus: a 1.6-litre four-cylinder Ford-

SPECIFICATIONS	Model Year 1974
Engine type:	**Ford/Lotus in-line 4-cyl**
Capacity/power:	**1.6 litres/126bhp**
Top speed (mph):	**121**
0–60mph (secs):	**6.7**

based unit with Lotus's own Twin Cam cylinder head and two twin-choke Weber carburettors. Even its original 105bhp was enough to give the lightweight Elan a top speed of 115mph and 0–60mph in 8.7 seconds, while the final Big Valve versions in the 1974 Elan Sprint had 126bhp, reducing 60mph to 6.7 seconds and boosting top speed to 121mph. It was available complete or in kit form. Although it had the then typical Lotus shortcomings, including a rather snug cockpit and marginal build quality, with its superbly developed suspension, brakes and steering, it was a great car and a commercial success.

Lotus Cortina MkI

Dates built: 1963–66

The image of Jim Clark three-wheeling a Lotus Cortina around the race tracks of Europe is the quintessential image of saloon car racing in the early 1960s. The Cortina started life as a family saloon, and Ford's enthusiasm for performance and Colin Chapman's engineering turned it into an icon. Putting the new 1.6 Lotus Twin Cam engine (from the Elan) under the bonnet gave a huge leap to 105bhp, taking top speed to 107mph and 0–60mph down to 13.5 seconds – which was dynamite for an early 1960s tin-top. That was the easy bit. Chapman added improved rear axle location with an A-frame and coil springs instead of leaf springs (although they reappeared later),

SPECIFICATIONS	Model Year 1965
Engine type:	**Ford/Lotus in-line 4-cyl**
Capacity/power:	**1.6 litres/105bhp**
Top speed (mph):	**107**
0–60mph (secs):	**13.5**

lowered the front strut suspension, fitted a close-ratio gearbox, plus improved brakes, wide wheels and a boot-mounted battery to improve the weight distribution. Inside there were additional instruments, a spidery woodrim wheel and new seats. Outside were front quarter bumpers, Lotus badges and the distinctive white paintwork with green stripes. As a racer, the Lotus Cortina was a giant killer, and as a road car it was much the same. Its early handling was slightly suspect and later cars put on weight, but they never lost their magic.

Lotus Elise

Dates built: 1996–on

In 1996, the mid-engined Elise brought Lotus back to its roots, with a small, affordable, innovative and brilliantly drivable sports car. The styling of its composite body was certainly distinctive and the interior was sparsely trimmed and uncompromisingly sporty. The open two-seater Elise was one of the best-handling cars in the world. Its secret was an innovative aluminium chassis, made using a new extrusion process to form many of its components and bonded, rather than welded, together. The result

SPECIFICATIONS	Model Year 1996
Engine type:	**in-line 4-cyl**
Capacity/power:	**1.8 litres tc/118bhp**
Top speed (mph):	**126**
0–60mph (secs):	**5.8**

was both light and super-stiff. Suspension used wishbones all round, brakes were all discs, steering was non-assisted and the Elise had an unmatched blend of grip with supple ride, sensational handling and pure feel. It didn't have huge power but its light weight made the most of what it had. The original engine was the Rover 1.8-litre 118bhp four from the MGF, which gave a top speed of almost 126mph and 0–60mph in 5.8 seconds. There was a limited edition Sport 135 option, and in 1999 Lotus added the Elise 111S, with 143bhp Rover VVC engine, close-ratio five-speed gearbox and better top-end performance, including over 130mph and 0–60mph in 5.3 seconds. There was also a track version with 190bhp available.

Lotus Esprit V8 Sport 350

Dates built: 1999–on

The V8 Sport 350 is the latest in the long Esprit line, and the fastest to date. Approaching its fourth decade, the Esprit always sat on the supercar margins but had an appeal of its own. The S1, launched in the mid-1970s, had a four-cylinder engine of adequate power but limited character (although James Bond did get a turbocharged version). The latest V8 generation has masses of both. In the Sport 350, the all-alloy four-cam 32-valve 3.5-litre twin-turbo V8 delivers 350bhp as in the V8 SE, but the Sport 350 adds lightness. The figure-hugging seats are racecar thin, and the 350 has the lightest possible magnesium wheels, with huge but ultra-lightweight racing brakes on lightweight alloy hubs. The carbonfibre rear wing is derived from a racing car and mounted on superlight alloy

SPECIFICATIONS	Model Year 1999
Engine type:	**V8**
Capacity/power:	**3.5 litres/350bhp**
Top speed (mph):	**175**
0–60mph (secs):	**4.5**

supports. Saving 80kg over the V8 SE, the Sport 350 takes top speed to 175mph and 0–60mph down to 4.5 seconds, with 100mph in only 10.1 seconds. The rear tyres are the biggest and suspension the stiffest on any Esprit, and the Esprit SE was already one of the sharpest-handling cars around – this one is even better.

Maserati 3500GT

Dates built: 1957–64

Like arch-rival Ferrari, Maserati started life in motor racing and then started to build road cars, first in limited numbers to fund the racers, and eventually more seriously. The 3500GT, launched in 1957, marked a transition, with road cars taking over from an ailing racing side. It was a classic front-engined rear-drive Grand Tourer, bodied as a coupé by Touring or as a convertible by Vignale. It was handsome, rugged and fast. Its tubular chassis carried coils and wishbones at the front, a live axle on leaf springs at the rear, a four-speed (later

SPECIFICATIONS	Model Year 1962
Engine type:	**in-line 6-cyl**
Capacity/power:	**3.5 litres/235bhp**
Top speed (mph):	**140+**
0–60mph (secs):	**7.8**

five-speed) gearbox and drum brakes all round, later replaced by discs. The light-alloy 3.5-litre twin-cam straight-six was derived from a sports racing engine, detuned slightly (but not much) for reasonable road manners with big performance. Power started at 220bhp and improved to 235bhp with the fuel-injected 3500GTI in 1962, for a maximum of over 140mph and 0–60mph in less than 8 seconds. And while the original 3500GT designation lasted until 1964, the basics of the car continued into a shorter-wheelbase coupé, the Sebring, in 1962, and the coupé/convertible Mistral in 1963 – carrying the 3500 line through the 1960s.

Maserati Ghibli

Dates built: 1966–73

Launched in 1966, the Ghibli continued a Maserati tradition for big, powerful, relatively simple but ruggedly engineered and often underrated front-engined GT cars. In either fastback or rare open forms, it was famous first for its stunning looks, penned by the young chief stylist at Ghia, Giorgietto Giugiaro. It was named after an African wind, and went like one. It was a big car, sharing its panelled tubular chassis, wishbone/live-axle suspension and all-disc brakes with the Quattroporte four-door 'saloon' and the Mexico 2+2, albeit shortened by a few inches for

SPECIFICATIONS	Model Year 1970
Engine type:	**V8**
Capacity/power:	**5.0 litres/355bhp**
Top speed (mph):	**154**
0–60mph (secs):	**6.8**

the two-seater Ghibli. There was a choice of five-speed manual or three-speed automatic transmissions, and where Ferrari and Lamborghini both had a tradition of V12s, the Ghibli used a version of Maserati's excellent all-alloy four-cam V8. In the Ghibli's original 4.7-litre form it gave 340bhp, and from 1970, stretched to 5 litres, it had 355bhp. More importantly, it was then able to meet more stringent American emissions regulations. In Europe, either version would nudge 155mph, with 0–60mph in less than 7 seconds. As a car with looks, luxury and performance, it was one of the greatest of Maseratis.

Maserati Bora

Dates built: 1971–80

In 1971, Maserati, which had generally been the
supercar bridesmaid among the Italian big three,
launched a car to rival Ferrari and Lamborghini's
best, in everything except, perhaps, an extrovert
image. It was the fruit of a better financial
position for Maserati now that they were backed
by the Citroën group, and it showed what they
could do given the chance. The Bora was named,
like many of Maserati's production sports cars,
for a fierce European wind, and it was a typically
rugged Maserati, with more than typically
exceptional performance. It had a mid-mounted
four-cam V8 of 4.7 litres and 310bhp and,
although it was no lightweight with its strong
construction, it could reach 60mph in 6.5 seconds
on its way to a 160mph maximum. What's more,
it was an unusually practical and uncomplicated

SPECIFICATIONS	Model Year 1971
Engine type:	**V8**
Capacity/power:	**4.7 litres/310bhp**
Top speed (mph):	**160**
0–60mph (secs):	**6.5**

supercar. It had a leather-trimmed interior,
reasonable luggage space, good soundproofing,
adequate visibility, even electric windows and
air-conditioning. It had Citroën's over-sensitive
but hugely powerful high-pressure brakes and
Citroën-derived hydraulically adjustable pedals
and seat height. It was compact by the standards
of its V12 compatriots, and had delightfully
balanced and forgiving handling, all of which
made it a superb but underrated gem.

Maserati 3200GT

Dates built: 1998–on

By the end of the 1990s, Maserati was a stablemate of Ferrari within the Fiat group, but with its new offering in 1998, the 3200GT, Maserati proved that it could still make cars with a character and an excellence of their own, at half the price of Ferrari's big guns. Styled by Giugiaro, the two-door 3200GT coupé was a generously roomy 2+2, beautifully trimmed in high-quality leather, and extremely stylish inside in spite of using several off-the-shelf Fiat components. It was a conventional front-engined, rear-drive car,

SPECIFICATIONS	Model Year 1998
Engine type:	**V8**
Capacity/power:	**3.2 litres/370bhp**
Top speed (mph):	**165**
0–60mph (secs):	**5**

with that long-time Maserati trademark, an all-
alloy four-cam V8. This one is 3.2 litres with four
valves per cylinder and twin turbos. It produces
370bhp, good for almost 165mph and 0–60mph
in 5 seconds, but with slightly ferocious mid-
range manners as the turbochargers push the
power through with a huge rush. Suspension is all
coil and wishbone, brakes are all ventilated, cross-
drilled discs, the 3200GT uses a six-speed manual
gearbox and steering is very quick rack and
pinion, which suits the car's agile handling,
although, like the 3200GT's low-speed ride, it
isn't quite as good as the latest gems from its
more illustrious cousin.

Mazda RX-7

Dates built: 1978–on

Almost alone in the industry, Mazda has persevered with Wankel rotary engines alongside its conventional piston engines, and created one of the world's more exciting sports cars in the RX-7. The first generation, launched in 1978, was interesting but, engine aside, not very sophisticated. The second generation, from 1985 to 1991, added improved rear suspension. The third generation, from 1991, became a minor supercar. It learned many lessons

SPECIFICATIONS	Model Year 1992
Engine type:	**twin-rotor Wankel**
Capacity/power:	**1.3 litres/237bhp**
Top speed (mph):	**156**
0–60mph (secs):	**6.0**

from Mazda's rotary-powered 1991 Le Mans winner, in particular the elimination of unwanted weight. The twin-rotor engine with a nominal capacity of 1308cc and twin turbos had plenty of power, with 237bhp; now the front-engined rear-drive car went on a diet, losing weight from the engine, the steel body/chassis unit, the all-wishbone suspension, even the wheels and tyres. What weight remained was superbly distributed, almost precisely 50/50 front and rear, and the use of a clever light alloy beam between five-speed gearbox and rear axle, plus solid suspension subframes, made a very stiff platform for exceptionally sharp handling. And with a top speed of 156mph and 0–60mph in 6 seconds, the RX-7 was as quick as it was lithe and sporty.

McLaren F1

Dates built: 1994–98

There is no arguing the pinnacle of the fast car world. The McLaren F1 has no rivals and, although there are often rumours of pretenders, from Ferrari in particular, to date nothing has approached the McLaren's peaks. These included a measured maximum speed of more than 231mph, perhaps more than 240mph, and a 0–60mph time of 3.2 seconds. To do that the McLaren's designer, former Grand Prix designer Gordon Murray, gave the F1 maximum power in minimum weight and the smallest possible package. The 6.1-litre four-cam 48-valve V12 developed by BMW's racing department produced 627bhp, in a car weighing only 1100kg. To achieve this weight both the chassis and body were made of carbonfibre and a catalogue of other exotic lightweight materials, plus racing-

SPECIFICATIONS	Model Year 1994
Engine type:	**BMW V12**
Capacity/power:	**6.1 litres/627bhp**
Top speed (mph):	**231+**
0–60mph (secs):	**3.2**

car-inspired design. The choice of a big, non-turbocharged engine ensured instant responses and sledgehammer performance whatever the circumstances. Taken together with the mid-mounted engine, hugely sophisticated chassis and suspension design, and giant brakes, these features gave the F1 all the abilities that helped the race-prepared version win Le Mans in 1995. Even the central driving position and lightweight luxury interior were uniquely focused on absolute drivability. The greatest supercar of all can really only be the McLaren.

Mercedes-Benz 300SL 'Gullwing'

Dates built: 1954–57

The 300SL, universally known as the Gullwing, was arguably the first modern supercar. It was fast, stylish and ultra-exclusive. The Gullwing nickname refers to the famous doors, which open upwards from the centre line of the roof, and look just like the wings of a bird. They were necessary because, where normal doors would be, the 300SL had deep, wide sills, concealing a complex spaceframe chassis similar to the racing sports car that was the 300SL's inspiration. The road car was built at the suggestion of American importer Max Hoffman, to capitalise on the 300SL racer's successes in the Carrera Panamericana and at Le Mans. It was virtually a money-no-object 'ultimate' road car when it was launched in 1954. It had a 3-litre straight-six

SPECIFICATIONS	Model Year 1954
Engine type:	**in-line 6-cyl**
Capacity/power:	**3.0 litres/240bhp**
Top speed (mph):	**155**
0–60mph (secs):	**6.0**

engine, pioneering fuel injection for production cars, giving 240bhp, a top speed approaching 160mph and 0–60mph in 6 seconds, which were almost unbelievable for a road car in the mid 1950s. It was also beautifully trimmed and pretty comfortable, although its handling, with twin-axle rear suspension, was tricky at high speeds, and its giant finned aluminium drum brakes only just matched the massive performance. However, flaws and all, the 300SL became a legend.

Mercedes-Benz CLK-GTR

Dates built: 1998–on

The CLK-GTR was one of the great exponents of a 1990s phenomenon: the Le Mans-style racing car specially manufactured for use on the road. However, where several of the major manufacturers produced roadgoing $1 million one-off replicas of their Le Mans racers (the price limit was set by the rules), the Mercedes-Benz CLK-GTR became a 'production' model of which 25 examples were planned, at an unrestricted price of around £1.1 million. It was built by Mercedes' partner AMG and was closely related to the 1997 race car. It has a 6.9-litre version of the 1997 four-cam 48-valve racing V12 rather

SPECIFICATIONS	Model Year 1999
Engine type:	**V12**
Capacity/power:	**6.9 litres/612bhp**
Top speed (mph):	**200 (limited)**
0–60mph (secs):	**3.8**

than the later 5-litre V8 turbo, but it musters an enormous 612bhp and an incredible soundtrack. It drives through a six-speed gearbox with racing-style paddle changes behind the steering wheel. In the low, lightweight, composite-shelled coupé, that gives a top speed electronically limited to exactly 200mph, with 0–60mph in 3.8 seconds. In addition, the CLK-GTR is also a fully equipped road car. It may be fast, noisy and nervously throttle-sensitive, but it is also reasonably smooth mechanically and fully equipped, with dual airbags, smart tartan cloth and leather trim, ABS, anti-skid control, a CD player and even air-conditioning. It is a 200mph style statement.

Mercedes-Benz AMG E55

Dates built: 1999–on

The E55, prepared by Mercedes' tuning partner
AMG, is the motoring equivalent of speaking
softly and carrying a big stick. At first glance it
looks like any other late 1990s E-Class, smooth
and sophisticated with its four-headlamp face –
the archetypal executive limo. However, look
closely and you'll notice that the wheels are
suspiciously bigger and the body sits a bit lower.
Look inside and you'll find only a few cosmetic
tweaks (even the familiar five-speed automatic
gearshift is still there), but take a peek under the
bonnet and you'll find the secret: the AMG-
prepared 5.5-litre 24-valve V8 engine producing
354bhp and huge torque for maximum mid-range
flexibility. This is a big, weighty car, but even so
the E55 is electronically limited to 155mph, and
hits 60mph in a sports-car-quick 5.5 seconds.

SPECIFICATIONS	Model Year 1999
Engine type:	**V8**
Capacity/power:	**5.5 litres/354bhp**
Top speed (mph):	**155 (limited)**
0–60mph (secs):	**5.5**

However, it retains most of its autobahn-cruiser character, of understated quality and refinement, and its massive performance comes easily and without vices. Body control is much tauter than on an ordinary E-Class and, although you could never call it nimble, with big rubber and the safety net of electronic stability control, the E55 is one big executive car with a very surprising sting in the tail.

Mercedes-Benz AMG ML55

Dates built: 1999–on

Alongside its other fast cars for Mercedes in the 1990s, perhaps AMG's strangest performance project was the ML55 – the world's fastest off-roader. Based on Mercedes' very successful M-Class 4x4, it swopped V6 power for V8 power and became a different car entirely. The V8 was a version of the one in the E55 saloon – four camshafts, four valves per cylinder and 350bhp, which even in a relative heavyweight like the M-Class was enough to promise a top speed of 147mph and 0–60mph in 6.8 seconds. It also, of course, retained the M-Class's sophisticated four-wheel-drive system, but it gained uprated brakes and suspension and a range of electronic safety features, including the ESP Electronic Stability Programme, and Mercedes' electronically controlled 4-ETS all-wheel-drive

SPECIFICATIONS	Model Year 1999
Engine type:	**V8**
Capacity/power:	**5.5 litres/350bhp**
Top speed (mph):	**147**
0–60mph (secs):	**6.8**

traction control system. With big five-spoke alloy wheels and wide high-speed-rated low-profile tyres, it promised maximum on-road grip with good ride comfort and real high-speed cruising ability. It also had an up-market trim package of sports seats and additional instruments, and enough sporty exterior touches, including bonnet bulges and wide arches, to underline the message of a mud-plugger with muscle.

Mercer Type 35 Raceabout

Dates built: 1911–14

Bugatti made the type number 35 famous in
Europe in the 1920s and 1930s, but in the
United States type 35 was famous long before
that, on a different kind of sporting car – the
Mercer Raceabout. First introduced in the
States in 1911, the all-American 35R was a cross
between a racing car and a stripped-bare fast
tourer, but it was actually a lot closer to the
former. In fact, the Mercer Raceabout was one
of the first cars that could genuinely be called
a sports car, because that was what it was
specifically designed for: performance with a
dash of style. It had a 4.9-litre four-cylinder 55hp
T-head engine, in a strong but rudimentary
cart-sprung ladder chassis. It had a bonnet over
the engine, curving wings over the four artillery-
type wheels, an exposed petrol tank, a monocle

SPECIFICATIONS	Model Year 1911
Engine type:	**in-line 4-cyl**
Capacity/power:	**4.9 litres/55bhp**
Top speed (mph):	**70+**
0–60mph (secs):	**n/a**

windscreen on the long, exposed steering column,
two equally exposed seats and not a great deal
else. Except, of course, for lashings of style. It had
considerable performance for 1911. Mercer
guaranteed 70mph for the standard Raceabout,
and with minimum weight it could get there
pretty quickly – certainly more quickly than it
could stop, with its rear-only drum brakes. The
Raceabout had delightful steering, a quick and
easy gearchange, an awful ride and a lot of
gaudily painted, tail-sliding entertainment value.

Mini Cooper S

Dates built: 1963–on (with interruptions)

There haven't been many less likely fast cars than the Mini, which arrived in 1959 as an answer to the fuel crisis and became a legend. As an extraordinarily roomy four-seater with style but no styling, it was a slow seller until it became a fashion statement for the smart set of the Swinging Sixties and took off. It took off for racing and rallying too, its exceptional roadholding and agile handling more than making up for what it lacked in power. It was launched with a four-cylinder pushrod engine of only 848cc and 32bhp, but a whole industry sprang up offering go-faster goodies for the Mini, and even its makers, BMC, created their own sporty Mini with the help of racing car constructor John Cooper. From its launch in 997cc form in 1961, there have been many

SPECIFICATIONS	Model Year 1964
Engine type:	**in-line 4-cyl**
Capacity/power:	**1.3 litres/76bhp**
Top speed (mph):	**98**
0–60mph (secs):	**10.8**

versions of the Mini Cooper, and there still are. Suffice it to say the most famous of all was the 1275cc Cooper S, which had 76bhp, a top speed of around 98mph and 0–60mph in less than 11 seconds. It was a prolific race and rally winner, of course, but what it mostly won was almost forty years of fame.

Mitsubishi Lancer Evo RS

Dates built: 1998–on

At the beginning of the new millennium, rules like those that created the Lancia Stratos and Audi Sport quattro still exist in the world of rallying, and so do the 'homologation specials' that are produced to satisfy those rules. The current classic is the Mitsubishi Lancer and, like its earlier cousins, after the original came the evolutions. In the Lancer's case, the starting point was a four-door, four-seater saloon that gained a powerful in-line four-cylinder turbo engine in the front and rally-bred four-wheel drive. It gained

SPECIFICATIONS	Model Year 1999
Engine type:	**in-line 4-cyl**
Capacity/power:	**2.0 litres/330bhp**
Top speed (mph):	**140**
0–60mph (secs):	**4.2**

rally-car looks, too, with aerodynamic add-ons in the form of deep front and rear airdams, wide side skirts and high rear wings. Pumped-out arches cover enormous alloy wheels with sticky ultra-low-profile tyres and space for the largest possible competition disc brakes. Inside, there were sporty touches, but the look is essentially the same as that of the standard car. The performance, however, is anything but standard. In its 1999 form, the 2-litre Evo VI RS Sprint has 330bhp for a top speed of 140mph and 0–60mph in 4.2 seconds, but what makes the Lancer Evo one of the fastest cars in the world from point to point is the fact that behind the road-car face, it's simply a rally car.

Morgan Plus Eight

Dates built: 1968–on

Do not underestimate the Morgan Plus Eight. Behind the old-fashioned looks, the Plus Eight has very new-fashioned performance, so long as you don't expect it to ride and handle like a modern supercar, and don't mind a few flies in your teeth. The Plus Eight has been around for a long time, since the company experimented with a Rover V8 engine in a Plus 4 chassis in 1966 and put the fully developed result into production in 1968. It is a classic Morgan in every respect: hand-built with a hand-crafted body on an ash frame, mounted on a separate ladder chassis with traditional sliding-pillar front suspension and cart-sprung live rear axle. It has rack and pinion steering and front discs, but it is inescapably old-fashioned at heart. Only the performance isn't. From the early days of 3.5 litres and 160bhp, the

SPECIFICATIONS	Model Year 1998
Engine type:	**Rover V8**
Capacity/power:	**4.6 litres/220bhp**
Top speed (mph):	**128**
0–60mph (secs):	**6.0**

ubiquitous all-alloy V8 has grown in 1999 Plus Eight flagship form to 4.6 litres and 220bhp, giving almost 130mph and 6 seconds to 60mph. That feels massively quick in a car whose rock-hard ride and lively handling evoke cars genuinely as old as the Plus Eight looks. The world would be poorer without it.

Nissan Skyline GT-R V-spec

Dates built: 1989–on

The 1999 Skyline GT-R, even by supercar standards, is an unusual beast. It looks solid and muscular, but slightly old-fashioned, like a 1980s mid-range sports coupé to which some body-kit has been grafted. Beware, looks can be very deceptive. The Skyline GT-R is a technical *tour de force*: front-engined, four-wheel drive, with multi-link suspension all round, HICAS four-wheel steering and packed with electronic management.

The latest R34 is slightly smaller and lighter, has even bigger discs and calipers, a sixth gear, carbonfibre underbody, aerodynamic additions to reduce lift, and an even more sophisticated four-wheel-drive system – its computer-controlled torque distribution taking into account steering angle, throttle opening and cornering angles, and reacting positively and instantaneously. Power is

SPECIFICATIONS   Model Year 1999

Engine type:	**in-line 6-cyl**
Capacity/power:	**2.6 litres/266bhp+**
Top speed (mph):	**156**
0–60mph (secs):	**4.5**

from a twin-turbo twin-cam 24-valve 2.6-litre straight-six, officially delivering 266bhp, rumoured to be closer to 320bhp. The way the Skyline, especially in its most uncompromising V-spec, uses the power is legendary. 156mph and 4.5 seconds are the headline figures, but the Skyline GT-R's real character is in its massive grip and awesome handling balance – honed around the Nurburgring, where the original was the first production car ever to beat an 8-minute lap time. The latest is even quicker.

Plymouth Superbird

Date built: 1970 only

In the mid-1960s, the US muscle-car era started.
By the late 1960s, average speeds for 'stock' car
racing on the big ovals had passed 190mph, and
pressure on the big manufacturers to win on
Sunday and sell to a performance-obsessed
market on Monday was intense. Briefly Ford
stole the initiative from Chrysler, but Chrysler
was about to win it back. Its problem was
aerodynamics – critical at the speeds the
NASCAR cars were running. Its answer was the
range including the Dodge Charger Daytona and
Plymouth Superbird. Both used the distinctive
needle nose and high rear wing, and both
worked. The prototype Charger ran first, in 1969.
Within a week it lapped the proving-ground track
at 204mph, including a straightline maximum of
243mph. In April 1970 it went on sale as a limited

SPECIFICATIONS	Model Year 1970
Engine type:	**V8**
Capacity/power:	**7.2 litres/375bhp**
Top speed (mph):	**200+ in race trim**
0–60mph (secs):	**n/a**

edition, with a 7.2-litre 375bhp V8. The
Superbird followed in 1970, based on the
Plymouth Roadrunner and subtly different from
the Dodge. Chrysler sold almost 2000 for
homologation, and the Superbird became a
racetrack success. In November Chrysler set a
closed-circuit lap record of over 201mph that
survived for thirteen years, but the racing
authorities were starting to be frightened by such
speeds, and in 1971 lowered the capacity limit
and ended the era.

Porsche 356 Carrera

Dates built: 1955–64

In the early 1950s, the Carrera Panamericana was the world's toughest motor race. In 1952 and 1953 Porsche won the 1500 production class with their 356. In 1953 and 1954 they won the 1500 sports category with the 550 Spyder, in 1954 using a new four-cam flat-four air-cooled race engine. In 1955 Porsche launched a car to celebrate its successes, the 356A 1500GS Carrera. It adopted a mildly detuned version of the four-cam race engine and, although planned as a limited edition, it became a big seller. The 356A already had wider wheels and tyres and uprated suspension; the Carrera engine gave it 110bhp in 1500GS form and 115bhp in the lighter, more simply trimmed GT, creating 120mph cars that were the fastest in their class. In 1958 capacity was increased from 1498 to 1588cc as the engine

SPECIFICATIONS	Model Year 1962
Engine type:	**air-cooled flat-4**
Capacity/power:	**2.0 litres/130bhp**
Top speed (mph):	**125**
0–60mph (secs):	**8.5**

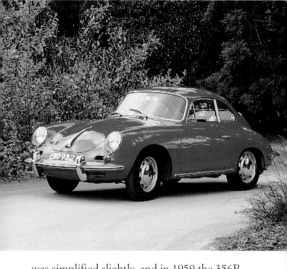

was simplified slightly, and in 1959 the 356B Carrera was introduced. Through 1960 and 1961 the 1600 engine was further uprated, and in 1962 Porsche launched the Carrera 2, fastest of all the 356 Carreras. Capacity was up to 1966cc, power to 130bhp, top speed to 125mph, and the Carrera 2 had Porsche's first production disc brakes. It was slightly wild, but wonderful.

Porsche 911 Carrera RS 2.7

Dates built: 1972–73

When the 911 appeared in 1963, the name
'Carrera' was already shorthand for performance,
but Porsche did not use the word lightly. It was
nine years before it appeared on a 911, and the
1972 911 Carrera RS 2.7 was an homologation
car, starting the 911's domination of sports car
racing for years to come. The production 911's
air-cooled flat-six engine was 2.4 litres, with up to
190bhp in the 911S. The Carrera RS was 2.7 litres
(as far as it could go without major redesign) and
power increased to 210bhp. It threw away all
surplus weight, used thinner steel in areas of the
shell, a glassfibre engine cover, thinner glass,
minimal sound insulation, no rear seats and
racing-type lightweight front seats. The even
lighter RSR, for racing, had aluminium doors and
bonnet, and more power. All had bigger wheels

SPECIFICATIONS	Model Year 1972
Engine type:	**air-cooled flat-6**
Capacity/power:	**2.7 litres/210bhp**
Top speed (mph):	**150**
0–60mph (secs):	**5.0**

and tyres, five-speed gearboxes, uprated brakes and suspension, and aerodynamic tweaks including the distinctive 'ducktail' spoiler. The roadgoing RS 2.7 became the fastest car in Germany, with a maximum speed of 150mph and 0–60mph in around 5 seconds; an RSR would exceed 170mph, with 0–60mph in 4 seconds or less. It was the beginning of a legend.

Porsche 911 Turbo

Dates built: 1974–on

The 1974 Porsche Turbo was another reinvention of the 911, a supercar in fact. The 911 was quick and highly respected, and the Turbo was another huge leap, focused on racing. At the time, turbocharging was established in racing, not least on Porsche's truly mighty 1000bhp Can-Am series racing cars, but it was still a rarity on production cars. Porsche experimented with it on a 1973 2.7 911, previewed a road car at the 1973 Paris Motor Show, launched a 500bhp turbocharged 911 racer early in 1974, and showed the production Turbo later that year.

Its role was to homologate the racer, but unlike the stripped-bare Carrera RS, the Turbo was a luxuriously equipped high-price model that depended more on power than lightness to achieve its speed. The 3-litre flat-six, with one

SPECIFICATIONS	Model Year 1976
Engine type:	**air-cooled flat-6**
Capacity/power:	**3.0 litres/260bhp**
Top speed (mph):	**155+**
0–60mph (secs):	**5.5**

big turbocharger, fuel injection and electronic
ignition, was good for 260bhp and gave an
enormously wide power spread that required
only four gears, albeit with some turbo lag. But
when the boost did arrive, nothing could match
the 911 Turbo. 60mph appeared in under 6
seconds, top speed was more than 155mph and
mid-range performance was colossal. All parts
were upgraded to match; wheels and tyres,
suspension, brakes, aerodynamics, all evolved. So
did the Turbo, to 3.3 litres and 300bhp by 1978,
and 330bhp by 1986.

Porsche 959

Dates built: 1987–88

The 959 was perhaps the most technically sophisticated supercar ever. Previewed in the Gruppe B concept car at the 1983 Frankfurt Show, it developed into a winning rally car, and appeared as a limited-production car in 1987. It was 911-based and bristled with technology. The muscular good looks were dictated by aerodynamics. The twin-turbo 2.8-litre flat-six was closely related to Porsche's Le Mans engines, with water-cooled heads and turbos, and 450bhp. There was a six-speed gearbox, racecar-derived brakes, and the 959's suspension featured self-levelling and a choice of

SPECIFICATIONS	Model Year 1987
Engine type:	**air/water-cooled flat-6**
Capacity/power:	**2.8 litres/450bhp**
Top speed (mph):	**201**
0–60mph (secs):	**3.7**

firmness and ride height, dropping automatically at high speed for stability and low drag. Four-wheel drive was electronically controlled to send power where it could be best used, with a driver-switchable option for traction modes to suit road conditions, including snow. There were two versions: the luxuriously equipped Comfort and the lighter, simpler Sport. Depending on the version, maximum speed fell either a couple of mph under or a couple over 200mph, making the 959 the first-ever 200mph production car, notwithstanding a 0–60mph time of 3.7 seconds and 0–100mph in 8.3 seconds. Most amazingly, the 959 was as usable as any other 911.

Porsche 911 GT1

Dates built: 1996–on

This was the ultimate development of the first 911 generation, and, although you have to look closely to find them, it genuinely has 911 parts under the skin. It satisfied 1990s Le Mans rules, which allowed extreme cars, within a capacity limit, so long as there was a 'road car' version, sold for less than $1 million. All the main contenders complied. The GT1 ran to more cars than most, because as well as the obligatory road cars Porsche sold several customer racing cars, all closely related to the works racer that won Le Mans in 1998.

The first GT1, in 1996, was ostensibly first-generation 911. Around a standard 911 front-chassis section, Porsche grafted a carbonfibre and Kevlar tub and body, on a stretched wheelbase, with an aerodynamic long nose and

SPECIFICATIONS	Model Year 1996
Engine type:	**water-cooled flat-6**
Capacity/power:	**3.2 litres/544bhp**
Top speed (mph):	**192 (limited)**
0–60mph (secs):	**3.7**

tail, no rear window and roof-mounted air
intake. The GT1 generated positive downforce at
speed and had racing suspension, brakes and
enormous 18-inch wheels. The flat-six was a
water-cooled 3.2-litre with twin-turbos, four
cams and four-valves per cylinder. The engine
produced 544bhp in a car weighing far less than
a normal 911, giving the roadgoing GT1 an
electronically limited maximum of 192mph and
0–60mph in 3.7 seconds. It was a racer with a
tax-disc.

Porsche 911

Dates built: 1997–on

In 1997, 34 years after it debuted, Porsche did the unthinkable and replaced the 911 – but only with a new generation 911. It was inevitable, to meet safety and emissions rules that had moved on more than thirty years and that the old 911 would ultimately fall behind. Officially it is type 996, spiritually it is 911. It looks different – smoother, a bit longer in nose and tail, less aggressive – but it is unmistakably of 911 genes.

It is more conventional and refined inside, and roomier and built for long-distance comfort, again underlaid with 911 character. It retains a four-cam, four-valve flat-six, rear-mounted but now water-cooled, to be more compact, more efficient and meet modern emissions and noise requirements. In 3.4-litre non-turbo form it develops 300bhp, keeping the new 911 in old 911

SPECIFICATIONS	Model Year 1997
Engine type:	**water-cooled flat-6**
Capacity/power:	**3.4 litres/300bhp**
Top speed (mph):	**174**
0–60mph (secs):	**4.8**

performance territory, at 174mph maximum and 0–60mph in under 5 seconds. Its character is a bit softer, but not by much. Steering, brakes and handling retain a classic 911 balance, and the 911 is still a very practical supercar, with docile temperament, adequate luggage space, excellent visibility and even room for two tolerant passengers. And of course, the evolution soon started again.

Renault 5 Turbo 2

Dates built: 1981–85

The Turbo 2 was the 1985 rebirth of a concept first aired for rallying in 1981, the mid-engined Renault 5 that won that year's Monte Carlo Rally, exactly as intended. On a slippery event, that turbocharged rear-drive car beat the new breed of four-wheel-drive rally cars largely because of its small size and agility. As a 'production' car (for homologation), the 1400 four-pot turbo engine gave 160bhp and a top speed of 125mph with 0–60mph in 6.7 seconds. It was handbuilt and the main contribution from the ordinary front-engined front-drive 5 was the basic shape, although even that was hardly recognisable under the huge wheelarches, airscoops and spoilers. It had many plastic and aluminium panels, all-wishbone suspension, ventilated discs all round, and drove through a five-speed transaxle from the

SPECIFICATIONS	Model Year 1985
Engine type:	**in-line 4-cyl**
Capacity/power:	**1.4 litres/158bhp**
Top speed (mph):	**125**
0–60mph (secs):	**6.9**

larger Renault 30 saloon, with engine and gearbox where the rear seats used to be. The 1985 Turbo 2 was even less ashamedly a competition-orientated car, with longitudinal mounted mid-engine. In special-bodied off-the-shelf competition form up to 240bhp was on tap, but surprisingly, the mid-engined 5 was also a reasonably refined, reasonably comfortable, entirely usable road car.

Renault Alpine GTA Turbo

Dates built: 1985–95

The Renault Alpines of the 1980s and 1990s
continued the links started in the 1950s, adding
refinement to performance and personality. The
plastic-bodied rear-engined Alpine V6GT and V6
Turbo line (dubbed Renault GTA in the UK)
began in 1984, the Turbo arriving a year later,
sharing the distinctive high-tailed, long-nosed,
slab-sided look. It had a steel backbone chassis,
wishbones all round and either a 2.8-litre 160bhp
Renault V6 or a 2.5-litre 200bhp turbocharged
one. It was roomy and comfortable, with safe,
communicative handling, and the Turbo had a
top speed of 150mph and 0–60mph in 6 seconds.
In 1991 it improved again with the launch of a
heavily revised successor to the GTA in the V6
turbo-engined Alpine A610. It echoed a special
edition from 1990, the GTA Le Mans, which had

SPECIFICATIONS	Model Year 1985
Engine type:	**V6 turbo**
Capacity/power:	**2.5 litres/200bhp**
Top speed (mph):	**150**
0–60mph (secs):	**6.0**

bigger wheels and tyres and revised bodywork. The A610 introduced a rounder, deeper nose and neat pop-up headlamps. It had a stiffer chassis with better weight distribution, improved brakes and suspension, special Michelin tyres and more power and performance. A 3-litre capacity liberated 250bhp, for almost 160mph and 0–60mph below 6 seconds – until the end of the line in 1995.

Renault Clio V6 Sport Trophy

Dates built: 1999–on

The Renault Clio V6 Sport Trophy was purely and simply a racing car, albeit a foretaste of a closely related 250bhp mid-engined Clio road car that followed in the year 2000. The V6 Sport Trophy looked like a normal Clio on steroids. The bodywork is the Clio equivalent of the old Turbo 5. Although based on the Clio II's three-door shell, it's low and wide with huge wheelarches and big spoilers both at the front and the rear. The wheelbase is stretched, and in the middle of the stripped-out single-seat shell (which is heavily braced by a complex built-in roll cage) sits an all-alloy Renault 3-litre V6

SPECIFICATIONS	Model Year 1999
Engine type:	**V6**
Capacity/power:	**3.0 litres/285bhp**
Top speed (mph):	**156**
0–60mph (secs):	**n/a**

engine, mounted with a six-speed transaxle gearbox. The gearshift is one-touch sequential, through a tall, robust lever that is set close to the tiny steering wheel on its long, exposed column. The plumbed-in fire control system is pure racing car, as are the rock-solid suspension, the 18-inch wheels and brake discs the size of dustbin lids. The engine is set in a completely bare shell and is virtually unsilenced – it is unbelievably noisy. However, performance and handling are instantaneous and super-twitchy respectively, and the car can reach a maximum of around 156mph, with staggering acceleration and braking power. The mid-engined Clio road car should be more luxurious … and quieter.

Toyota Supra

Dates built: 1993–on

The late-lamented 1990s Toyota Supra has been described as the last of a generation of Japanese fast GTs. In fact, it was perhaps the fastest of them all. To succeed against Japanese rivals like the Mazda RX-7, Mitsubishi 3000GT and Nissan 300ZX, it had to be. It was a curvaceous yet subliminally muscular two-door coupé, its intentions spelled out by wide wheelarches, deep airdams and high rear wing. It was front-engined, rear-drive and beautifully engineered. It embraced lightness, and actually weighed less than its less powerful predecessor. It used aluminium for much of its

SPECIFICATIONS	Model Year 1998
Engine type:	**in-line 6-cyl**
Capacity/power:	**3.0 litres/326bhp**
Top speed (mph):	**156 (limited)**
0–60mph (secs):	**5.1**

all-wishbone suspension, its engine mountings
and bonnet. Elsewhere it used high-strength low-
weight plastics, and did without anything it did
not strictly need. That left it with twin airbags,
ABS, traction control, big wheels and tyres, and
even air-conditioning in the otherwise ordinary
cockpit. However, there was nothing ordinary
about its electronically limited 156mph maximum
or 0–60mph in 5.1 seconds, with massive mid-
range flexibility. That came from a twin-cam 24-
valve 3-litre straight-six pushing out 326bhp
through a six-speed gearbox and torque-sensing
differential, and the grippy, responsive chassis
was as good as the rest.

TVR Cerbera

Dates built: 1996–on

In the 1990s, the small TVR company finally found commercial success, and, after years of splendid sports cars, made a spectacular supercar, the Cerbera coupé. It followed and improved on the established TVR formula of shoehorning big power into a relatively simple chassis and clothing it in a jaw-droppingly original glassfibre shell. The Cerbera, even by TVR's standards, looks aggressive and unique; the interior, with its complex scatter of instruments and sweeping shapes, is just as dramatic. There are nominal rear seats, letterbox-slot rearward visibility, surprising comfort, tolerable refinement and massive

SPECIFICATIONS	Model Year 1999
Engine type:	**TVR/AJP8 V8**
Capacity/power:	**4.5 litres/420bhp**
Top speed (mph):	**170+**
0–60mph (secs):	**3.9**

performance. The 350bhp 4.2-litre V8 is fast and flexible; the version with TVR's own light and compact AJP8 V8 is fast and ferocious, thanks to 420bhp from a race-bred 4.5 litres. That gives more than 170mph and 0–60mph in 3.9 seconds, and the Cerbera is also the best-handling of 1990s TVRs, thanks to its longer wheelbase and the added stiffness of a fixed roof. You can have 350bhp with six cylinders in-line, from TVR's own twin-cam 4-litre engine in the Speed Six, which has a character all its own – at a price that makes Cerbera performance even more amazing.

Glossary

ABS: Anti-lock Braking System: sensors in the brakes sense impending skidding and prevent it, allowing greater control of the car.

axle: the metal shaft to which a car's wheels are attached.

bhp: 'brake horsepower', measurement of the power output of an engine, measured by a brake applied to the drive shaft.

cabriolet: traditionally a body style where part of the roof was open and part covered. Now often used synonymously with *convertible.*

calipers: part of disc-brake mechanism that forces the brake pads against the revolving brake disc.

cam/camshaft: cams are irregularly-shaped metal lobes on the camshaft which rotate

and so govern the opening and closing of the inlet and exhaust valves.

capacity: the volume of the cylinders in the engine. Larger capacity allows more power. Usually measured in cubic centimetres (cc) or litres and in the USA in cubic inches.

carburettor: mixes and controls delivery of fuel and air to the cylinders.

chassis: the frame around which the car is built.

compression: the piston's compression of the fuel mixture in the cylinder precedes its ignition and increases its explosive energy. Hence higher compression allows increased power, but often less flexibility.

convertible: car with a folding roof allowing conversion to 'open' motoring.

coupé: literally 'cut'. Short body style, usually applied to two-door sporty styles.

cylinder: the cylinder houses the piston and is where combustion takes place.

damper: see *shock absorber*.

differential: gear system which distributes drive to the driven road wheels. May also be referred to as 'final drive' or 'transaxle'.

disc brake: mechanism that uses pads to grip a revolving disc attached to the wheel to slow it. Generally more efficient than older-style drum brakes.

drag coefficient: a measure of air resistance or 'drag'.

drum brake: mechanism that forces a friction pad attached to a 'shoe' outwards against a drum-like housing attached to the revolving wheel.

emissions: the components of car exhaust gases harmful to the environment.

Formula 1 racing (F1): generally regarded as the highest class of single-seat car racing. There are many other classifications including Formula 3 and 3000.

four/five/six speed-gearbox: the number of forward gears available to the driver.

four-wheel-drive: in most cars power is distributed to just two wheels. With this system, it goes to all four, giving both extra traction and control.

GT/Gran Turismo: the Italian *Gran Turismo* was originally applied to high-speed luxury cars, as opposed to more spartan sports cars. But the shortened term GT is now often applied to many cars to convey an image of speed.

homologation: building a limited number of cars in order to qualify the car as eligible to compete in a 'production' racing class.

horsepower: measure of the engine's power output.

monocoque: one-piece body construction with no separate chassis.

overdrive: additional high-speed 'cruising' gear.

overhead cam: camshaft sits above the valves, allowing higher revving and more performance than if the camshaft is placed low in the engine.

pot: nickname for cylinder.

production car: a 'normal' car available to the general public, as opposed to racing cars, or limited-run 'specials'.

pushrod: rod transmitting the action of the cams to the valves.

rack and pinion steering: a pinion at the end of the

steering column engages with a 'rack' of teeth and causes the steering wheels to turn. Generally acknowledged to give good steering 'feel'.

rear drive: when power is delivered to the rear wheels of the car.

sequential gear shift: gear selector that allows the driver to move directly (and quickly) between gears rather than having to 'find' a gear, as with the conventional 'H'-pattern selector.

shock absorber: suspension component that controls the car's ride.

sump: pan at the bottom of the engine that holds oil for lubrication.

supercharger: pump driven off the engine that forces air and fuel into the engine under pressure, so allowing more power.

synchromesh: mechanism now found on virtually all gearboxes that synchronises the speed of gear wheels and makes for easy gear changes.

torque: measure of the turning power produced by the engine.

torsion bar: suspension component that controls wheel travel by means of a twisting rod.

traction: term referring to the 'grip' of the car on the road.

transmission: the system by which the power of the engine is delivered to the wheels.

transverse/longitudinal: transverse refers to components, such as the engine, positioned across the breadth of the car and longitudinal along the length of the car.

tub: strong central body structure to which outrigger frames are attached.

turbocharger: pump boosting the pressure at which the fuel and air mixture is delivered to the engine. The pump is powered by the engine's own exhaust gases, this cycle often resulting in a 'lag' before the performance effect from the turbo is felt.

V6/V8/V12 engine: refers to the cylinders being arranged in a 'V' formation as opposed to the more common in-line formation.

valve: the mechanism which allows the fuel mixture to flow into the cylinder and the exhaust gases to flow out. High-performance engines often have multi-valves per cylinder to increase the flow.

wheelbase: the distance between the front and rear wheels of the car.

wishbone: suspension layout where the wheel is attached at the apex of a pivoting triangular structure. Often found on racing cars.

COLLINS GEM
BABIES' names
a mine of information

COLLINS GEM
BEER
a mine of information

COLLINS GEM
BIRDS
a mine of information

COLLINS GEM
CALORIE Counter
a mine of information

COLLINS GEM
FACT FILE
a mine of information

COLLINS GEM
FENG SHUI
a mine of information

COLLINS GEM
FLAGS
a mine of information

COLLINS GEM
Healthy EATING
a mine of information

COLLINS GEM
QUOTATIONS
a mine of information

COLLINS GEM
SAS Self-Defence
a mine of information

COLLINS GEM
SAS Survival Guide
a mine of information

COLLINS GEM
SEASHORE
a mine of information

COLLINS GEM
TREES
a mine of information

COLLINS GEM
Understanding DREAMS
a mine of information

COLLINS GEM
WILD flowers
a mine of information

COLLINS GEM
WINE Dictionary
a mine of information